St. Edith Stein's Aesthetic

All genuine art is revelation and all artistic creation is sacred service.

The Science of the Cross

St. Edith Stein's Aesthetic

Beauty and Sanctity:
Masterpiece of the Divine Artist

Elizabeth A. Mitchell

GRACEWING

First published in England in 2025
by
Gracewing
2 Southern Avenue
Leominster
Herefordshire HR6 0QF
United Kingdom
www.gracewing.co.uk

No part of this publication may be reproduced,
stored in a retrieval system, or transmitted in any form
or by any means, electronic, mechanical,
photocopying, recording or otherwise,
without the written permission of the publisher.

The right of Elizabeth A. Mitchell to be identified as the author of
this work has been asserted in accordance with the Copyright,
Designs and Patents Act 1988.

© 2025 Elizabeth A. Mitchell

ISBN 978 085244 994 3

Typeset by Gracewing

Cover design by Bernardita Peña Hurtado

For the Blessed Mother

*May her daughter St. Teresa Benedicta of the Cross,
Edith Stein, be honored as a
Doctor of the Universal Church.*

Contents

Preface by Cardinal Raymond Leo Burke........................... xi

Introduction xv

1 A Life's Formation in Art.. 1
   The Early Years 1
   Adulthood and Conversion..7
   Faith and Carmel...14

2 The Living Image... 27
   The Image Stirs 27
   Stein as Living Image..37
   "We are Heading East" 46

3 The Soul's Awakening.. 55
   From Hollow Men to Soul-Filled Living.....................55
   Beauty and the Human Spirit 71
   The Revival of the Community...................................82

4 The Art of Sanctity.. 97
   Becoming God's Masterpiece......................................97
   Artist and Image..111
   The Divine Artist..120

Conclusion.. 135

Appendix 139
　Missa in Honorem B.M.V. Reginae Pacis 139
Bibliography 145

Preface

In this seminal work on the aesthetic of St. Edith Stein (Sister Teresa Benedicta of the Cross, O.C.D.), the author Dr. Elizabeth Mitchell, S.C.D., reconstructs for the first time the vision of art, beauty, and sanctity of this heroic martyr for the Catholic Faith. Insofar as her life witnessed to a courageous abandonment to the Truth and thus to a lived embrace of the Cross of Christ, Stein emphasizes the way in which each person, surrendered to Christ in doing the Father's will in all things, can become a living work of art, a masterpiece of God, the Divine Artist. Her life expressed the incomparable beauty of a "fellow worker [with Christ] in the truth" (2 Jn 8).

Scholars will appreciate, in particular, Mitchell's painstaking synthesis of Stein's corpus in the field of aesthetics, never systematically published by the saint during her lifetime and partly lost to posterity due to the climate of violence and chaos in which she lived and offered her life. Martyred in 1942 by the Nazis at Auschwitz during the Second World War, St. Teresa Benedicta of the Cross completed, in 1941, a year before her death, an investigation on symbolic theology and aesthetics. Stein's interest in aesthetics is first revealed in her 1917 doctoral investigation, *On the Problem of Empathy*. Throughout the intervening academic writings produced by Stein, and through her spiritual poetry and lived Carmelite spirituality, a picture emerges of a saint who understood the life of faith to be a creative collaboration with the Eternal Artist, dying to self to live solely for the Father in Christ through the outpouring of the Holy Spirit from His glorious-pierced Heart into her heart. In the words of Saint Paul, Christ weds Himself to us in the Church and offers Himself totally in sacrifice so that we, the Church, may be "in splendor ... without spot or wrinkle or any such thing ... holy and without blemish" (Eph 5, 27).

In this her study, *St. Edith Stein's Aesthetic: Beauty and Sanctity—Masterpiece of the Divine Artist*, Mitchell works shoulder to shoulder with St. Teresa Benedicta of the Cross, aligning fragments, analyzing letters and manuscripts, and interpreting and translating original texts. The work of St. Teresa Benedicta of the Cross in the sphere of aesthetics culminates in her final work, *The Science of the Cross*, in which she states, unequivocally, that "all genuine art is revelation, and all artistic creation is sacred service".[1] In fact, communion with Christ in His Eucharistic Sacrifice is the form of the Christian life, of the pursuit of divine truth and the living of truth in divine charity. To that end, the inclusion of St. Teresa Benedicta's original manuscript from the Cologne Carmel Archive of a *Mass in Honor of the Blessed Virgin Mary Queen of Peace*, assists the reader to offer sacred worship, to make an offering of self, through, with, and in Christ, to the glory of God and for the salvation of the world.

In the end, the Church in today's world faces the challenge of bringing the person of Christ ever more fully to those in need of hope, mercy, and eternal salvation. In Him alone is our hope, mercy, and eternal salvation. The early Christian martyrs taught us the way of unflinching profession of faith before the tyrants of each age. Their example of a life offered, in complete trust, to Our Lord, no matter the diverse social milieux, moral aberrations, or political persecutions, has continued to inspire saintly witness throughout the history of the Church. Those early Christian martyrs inspired the first popes, missionaries, priests, religious, and faith-filled laity. From them, the Gospel spread through continuing witness to the farthest reaches of the globe, to bustling cities and remote villages, and even, in our modern epoch, to the gates of Auschwitz. This witness, handed on to us by courageous believers like St. Teresa Benedicta of the Cross, is now our sacred trust.

Preface

May this work, an unparalleled explication of the aesthetic of St. Edith Stein—woman, philosopher, cloistered Carmelite, and martyr—, one of the Catholic Church's brightest stars of holiness, make more available her legacy of beauty and holiness to many, uncovering for succeeding generations of the faithful a hitherto unmined facet of her intellectual and spiritual patrimony. In the name of all readers of her study, I thank wholeheartedly Dr. Elizabeth Mitchell for so wonderful a gift.

RAYMOND LEO CARDINAL BURKE
Trinity Sunday
June 15, 2025

Introduction

On a personal visit to the Carmel of Echt in the Netherlands, from which St. Edith Stein was arrested and deported to Auschwitz in 1942, the final hours leading up to Stein's death were retold to me by a nun familiar with her story. Sr. Catherine of the Word of God recounted that amidst the suffering and brutality of those harrowing days and hours, Stein offered constant assistance to the mothers and children arrested with her. She especially cared for the many young children whose mothers were too distraught to care for them properly.[2] Testimony upon testimony was later given of Stein's inner calm and outward charity:

> A Jewish prisoner who survived the war testified that Edith was "just like an angel, going around amongst the women, comforting them, helping them and calming them ... Edith took care of the little children, washed them and combed them, looked after their feeding and their other needs ... She followed one act of charity with another until everyone wondered at her goodness."[3]

In her final, selfless acts of love and compassion, Stein resembled a "living *Pietà*,"[4] the Echt sisters recounted. Just as Our Lady holds the broken body of Christ in Michelangelo's masterpiece, so Stein became a "*Pietà* ohne Christus, mit Kind," a "*Pietà* holding a child in the place of Christ."[5] Radiating compassion, love, and self-offering to the end, St. Edith Stein is for us a living image, a masterpiece of the Divine Artist. She is a living artwork that reveals the splendor of Christ to a darkened world through her heroic life and faith-filled death.

"All genuine art is revelation and all artistic creation is sacred service,"[6] Stein boldly proclaims in *The Science of the Cross*, her penetrating analysis of Christ's Cross as the defining truth of the life of St. John of the Cross. This *"science of the cross,"* she explains, "is not to be understood in the usual meaning of *science* ... but a living, real, effective truth."⁷ The manuscript of this spiritual opus, Stein's final gift to the world, was left out on her desk, in her cell in Carmel, when she was arrested and deported to Auschwitz concentration camp on 2 August 1942.⁸ A few brief days after her arrest, Stein would offer her life as a martyr of the Catholic Faith, gassed with other converts from Judaism to Catholicism in a small white farmhouse on edge of the prison camp.

The canonization of St. Teresa Benedicta of the Cross, Edith Stein, on 11 October 1998, brought the works of this brilliant intellect and courageous witness of the faith to the forefront of Catholic life and thought. Widely known by her secular name Edith Stein, this Jewish convert to Catholicism, philosopher, and Carmelite nun martyred in the death camps of Auschwitz, was subsequently named by Pope St. John Paul II as Co-patroness of Europe, on 1 October 1999. On this occasion, the Holy Father, himself a poet, playwright, and actor, who participated in the clandestine Rhapsodic Theater as a form of cultural resistance in Nazi-occupied Poland, referred to Stein as "the symbol of the dramas of Europe this century."⁹

Killed in such brutal conditions, silenced by the darkened hearts of men, what could Stein have to say to a spiritually diseased world about beauty, art, and sanctity? Are such things relevant to a humanity broken by sin? Does beauty have power? Is sanctity a visible quality? Can a life dedicated to artistic expression make a difference in the world? To all these demands, Stein answers a resounding yes, through her academic writings and with her life.

St. Edith Stein loved art and beauty, although she demurs being an aesthete in the strictest sense of the term. Writing from the Carmel of Cologne to a friend in 1935, she asserts:

> Despite the many reasons you give for your opinion that my verdict is to be taken into account, I want to reveal to you that it is a very inexpert verdict. I am neither an artist

nor a connoisseur, nor even—in the usual sense—an art lover. Certainly I have seen many a beautiful piece, and there are works I really like. But I have been always too much occupied with other matters to study art *ex professo* professionally.[10]

Sadly, Stein's comprehensive academic work on the themes of artistic creativity and personal formation has been lost to posterity. Many of Stein's letters were destroyed during her lifetime by the Carmel of Cologne as necessary protection from Nazi reprisal. Stein never completed some texts, and others are missing sections due to the difficult circumstances facing those entrusted with the preservation of her writings. Profound gratitude is due to the courageous individuals who safeguarded Stein's manuscripts under wartime conditions. Texts were spirited across patrolled borders, buried in the convent garden, unburied, stashed in bags during severe shelling, and salvaged from the rubble of bombarded buildings. Stein's first biographer, her novice director and then Mother Prioress of the Cologne Carmel, Sr. Teresia Renata Posselt, OCD, relates the heroic search for Stein's papers after upheaval:

> Eventually, in March 1945, a military vehicle, carrying Professor Father Hermann van Breda, OFM, director of the Husserl Archive and the Carmelite Prior of Greleen, went from Leuven to Echt, where Sr. Pia and Sr. Francisca had returned. There they searched for the manuscripts. Since they could find nothing, they drove on to Herkenbosch in ice-cold weather. They searched the tiny convent that was now nothing more than a ruin, and they found, soiled, torn, and scattered, about three quarters of (Sr. Benedicta's) papers.[11]

Researchers therefore face a patchwork of texts. We can glean Stein's ideas from reconstruction and interpretation. While some documents exist in their entirety, others have come to us as fragments. Other works simply have not surfaced or are resurfacing gradually.

Stein presents an analysis of art and the artist in her 1917 doctoral dissertation, *On the Problem of Empathy*. Her ultimate conclusions regarding artistry were lost when edited from her final draft. Stein intended her 1941 article on symbolic knowledge and aesthetics, entitled "Ways to Know God: The 'Symbolic Theology' of Dionysius the Areopagite and Its Objective Presuppositions," as a preliminary study to a larger investigation. She was dead less than one year later.

The artistic investigation never produced systematically by Stein, however, recurs throughout her writings. Stein views the world through the lens of the arts. Characters from novels populate her philosophical analogies. Strands of music uplift her darkest moments. Her thoughts on art and the formation of the human person, which reappear in various forms throughout her works, culminate in *The Science of the Cross*, left in manuscript form on her desk at the moment of her arrest in 1942. Her final work insists to us that artistic creativity is a "sacred service," and all genuine art is "revelation."[12] We can only hope that, with time, as much of Stein's work as possible will be brought to light.

Through the gracious assistance of Sr. M. Amata Neyer, OCD, curator of the Edith-Stein Archiv, Karmel Maria vom Frieden, in Cologne, Germany, one of St. Edith Stein's original manuscripts is offered within this study. The text, a *Mass in Honor of the Blessed Virgin Mary Queen of Peace*, composed by Stein in Latin and German, at the request of her religious superiors in Carmel, appears here for the first time in English translation, providing a poignant glimpse into Stein's reverence for the formative spirituality of liturgical beauty.[13]

Stein is in fact much more than an aesthete. She takes us to the center of the artwork and discloses to us the divine origin of the beauty revealed through the created work. The revelatory power of art lies in this sacred connection of every genuine artwork to its divine origin, God Himself. As Prof. John Saward affirms in his thought-provoking study *The Beauty of Holiness and the Holiness of Beauty*:

Introduction

> The uncontainable God has been sheltered, in the flesh, by the womb and arms of the Virgin. The human face of the eternal Son, lovelier beyond all others, does not elude all imaging, for human eyes have beheld its glory (cf. Jn 1:14; 1 Jn 1:1). The divine Word speaks in human words, sanctifying men's tongues for new poetic praise. He has brought to earth the songs of the halls of Heaven. The sacred art of His Church is, therefore, her delight and dogmatic duty.[14]

Our own lives, ultimately, are a living artwork, a material manifestation of the divine idea God conceives of each of us from all eternity. "Before I formed you in the womb, I knew You," He reveals (Jeremiah 1:5). Our lives are the handiwork of God, the Divine Artist. "We are God's Masterpiece," St. Paul proclaims, "created in Christ Jesus for good works, which God prepared beforehand, that we should walk in them" (Ephesians 2:10).

And yet, in forming the human person the Divine Artist does not work on inanimate material. In our development as His artwork, we have a say in the result. He molds our lives in cooperation with our free will and our accepting correspondence with His grace. The "eternal Artist"[15] who knows our perfect fulfillment calls forth our essence into realization. He crafts us into a masterwork if we consent. When we allow the Divine Artist to mold, shape, chisel, and finely brush stroke the details of our lives, we become the beautiful and resplendent artwork which He envisions. We become a living masterpiece of the Divine Artist.

Stein herself becomes such a masterpiece. Pope St. John Paul II celebrates her artistic culmination in his remarks at the symphony performed on the evening of Stein's canonization in Rome, in turn challenging us to become a living work of art:

> Edith Stein is an example and a guide for us. At the start, she too heard from afar just "a few faint notes" of the melody of God's mysterious plan. In the school of the

Cross, these sounds were later harmonized and became a whole symphony.

Through her intercession, may your lives too be transformed into a harmonious symphony to the praise and glory of God.[16]

In the stench of a cattle car, behind the barbed wire, devoid of freedom, with no earthly power and no assurance that her witness would have a lasting effect, Stein becomes a living image of surrender to the Cross of Christ. Her suffering radiates life and fruitfulness because God intends this denouement for Stein from all eternity. Stein's ultimate sacrifice is the final flourish of the Master's brush, allowed by her spirit in union with the Divine Artist.

Introduction

Notes

1. Edith Stein, *The Science of the Cross: A Study of St. John of the Cross*, trans. Josephine Koeppel, OCD, ed. Dr. L. Gelber and Romaeus Leuven, OCD, *The Collected Works of Edith Stein*, Vol. 6 (Washington, DC: ICS Publications, 2002) 12
2. Conversation with Schwester Katerina vom Wort Gottes (Sr. Catherine of the Word of God), of the Karmelitessen Klooster, Echt, the Netherlands, February 2002. Note: Throughout this text, Edith Stein, who as a Carmelite took the religious name Sister Teresa Benedicta of the Cross, will be referred to as "St. Edith Stein," or "Stein," following the colloquial usage of her secular name that has emerged since her canonization. See Pope St. John Paul II's canonization formula: "We declare and define that Blessed Teresa Benedicta of the Cross, Edith Stein, is a saint, and we enroll her among the saints," in *Holiness Befits Your House: Documentation on the Canonization of Edith Stein* (ICS Publications: Washington, DC, 2000) 7.
3. Cynthia Cavnar, *Meet Edith Stein* (Ann Arbor, MI: Servant Publications, 2002) 148. Interior quote from Teresa de Spiritu Sancto, *Edith Stein* (New York: Sheed and Ward, 1952) 217.
4. Conversation with Schwester Katerina vom Wort Gottes (Sr. Catherine of the Word of God), of the Karmelitessen Klooster, Echt, the Netherlands, February 2002.
5. Conversation with Schwester Katerina vom Wort Gottes (Sr. Catherine of the Word of God), of the Karmelitessen Klooster, Echt, the Netherlands, February 2002.
6. Stein, *Science*, 12.
7. Stein, *Science*, 9.
8. See Stein, *Science*, I.C.S. Introduction, 'Sr. Benedicta's manuscript *Science of the Cross* had not been returned to its place leading one to presume that she had it out and had been working on it that day,' xxxv.
9. Pope John Paul II, "Solemn Inauguration of the Special Assembly for Europe of the Synod of Bishops: Homily," n. 5, (1 October 1999).
10. Edith Stein, *Self-Portrait in Letters 1916–1942*, trans. Josephine Koeppel, OCD, ed. Dr. L. Gelber and Romaeus Leuven, OCD, *The Collected Works of Edith Stein*, Vol. 5 (Washington, DC: ICS Publications, 1993) Letter 199 to Hedwig Dülberg.
11. Teresia Renata Posselt, OCD, *Edith Stein: The Life of a Philosopher and Carmelite*, ed. Susanne M. Batzdorff, Josephine Koeppel, and John

12. Sullivan (Washington, DC: ICS Publications, 2005) 225.
12. Stein, *Science*, 12.
13. See Appendix. *Missa et Officium in Honorem B.V.M. Reginae Pacis*, Edith-Stein-Archiv, Karmel "Maria vom Frieden," Cologne, Germany. For the complete text of the *Missa et Officium in Honorem B.M.V. Reginae Pacis*, see Elizabeth A. Mitchell, S.C.D., *Artist and Image: Artistic Creativity and Personal Formation in the Thought of Edith Stein* (Memphis: St. Paul Institute, 2021) https://stpaulmemphis.com/product/the-artist-the-image/.
14. John Saward, *The Beauty of Holiness and the Holiness of Beauty: Art, Sanctity and the Truth of Catholicism* (San Francisco: Ignatius Press, 1997) 110.
15. Edith Stein, "I Am Always in Your Midst," from *The Hidden Life*, trans. Waltraut Stein, Ph.D., ed. Dr. L. Gelber and Michael Linssen, OCD, *The Collected Works of Edith Stein*, Vol. 4 (Washington, DC: ICS Publications, 1992) 119.
16. Pope John Paul II, "Address at Canonization Concert: Edith Stein Heard 'Melody' of God's Will," *L'Osservatore Romano*, October 14, 1998, Weekly Edition in English, no. 41.

1 A LIFE'S FORMATION IN ART

> What I read then of *belles lettres* provided me with treasure to last the rest of my life.
>
> Stein, *Life in a Jewish Family*[1]

St. Edith Stein, the resplendent master work whose life culminates in a self-offering with Christ's Cross in Auschwitz, was herself a life-long lover of art and beauty. She finds in the arts a "treasure" to enrich her entire life, and she refers to the great poets as her "intimate friends."[2] Her lifelong formation in art can be divided into three periods: the early years of childhood and adolescence, her adulthood and conversion, and the culminating period of faith and Carmel.

The Early Years

From her earliest childhood, Stein's alert and sensitive soul found in the arts a constant and beloved companion. Her own brothers and sisters first offered passage into this artistic world through the heroes, heroines, epic struggles, and triumphant songs which they brought home from school to the eager mind of their youngest sibling. In her autobiographical work *Life in a Jewish Family*, intended as a biography of her mother and a presentation of authentic Jewish life in the face of growing intolerance towards the Jewish people in Germany in the years leading up to the Second World War, Stein recounts a characteristic scene shared with her older brother Paul, when she was not yet six years old:

> While I clutched his hair, he could carry me around a room on his shoulders by the hour, tirelessly singing student or folk songs to me. To amuse us both, he used to show me all the pictures in his bulky history of literature

and asked me who or what was being represented; in his zeal he would cover the captions although at the time I was still unable to read.³

Stein also gave eager attention to her older sister Frieda's poetic recitations, absorbing this literary influence with rapidity and ease:

> (Frieda) enjoyed reciting aloud the poems she had to memorize for school. That way, I learned Schiller's and Uhland's ballads while I was still a small child, and at the age of five I could declaim "Bertran de Born" from memory.⁴

Such stimulants were certainly not wasted on such a bright and active young mind. Jean de Fabrégues tells us in *Edith Stein: Philosopher, Carmelite Nun, Holocaust Martyr*, "When the family played the game called 'Dichter-quartett,' the child of four amazed the guests because she knew the names of the authors and could match them with their works."⁵ Likewise, Stein's sister Erna notes that Edith "had an excellent memory and retained everything. Many of our numerous uncles and aunts would tease or try to confuse her by telling her that *Maria Stuart* was written by Goethe, or the like. This misfired with deadly certainty."⁶

Stein's early kinship with literature, experienced through Paul's lectures on Goethe and Frieda's recitation of verse, would soon deepen into a lifelong love, as the attentive listener became a voracious reader. Noting that "reading, in general, played a large role in our family," Stein recalls her traditional practice in which "the first thing in the morning, I would begin to read while my mother fixed my hair."⁷ She goes on to express the delight she experienced on high Jewish holy days, when her "greatest joy was to have unlimited time to read an enjoyable book. ... On this occasion reading in bed was permitted."⁸ In this familial environment, Stein began to store up that treasure which would later become a profound source of interior nourishment and strength.

Despite her love of reading, Stein voluntarily broke from formal schooling for a brief period during her teenage years. She had a very decisive temperament. The family often recalled how on the day of her sixth birthday, 12 October 1897, the middle of the school year notwithstanding, little Edith had demanded to go to school. Now, in 1906, at age 14, she had decided to discontinue her schooling. In her autobiography, Stein recounts the freedom which her mother gave to this decision, which was entirely Stein's own. "Leaving school was anything but difficult for me ... A healthy instinct was the decisive factor. It told me I had been sitting on a school-bench long enough and needed a change."[9]

In this scholastic interim Stein made her way to Hamburg to assist her older sister Else with the cares of raising a young family. Amidst her domestic duties Stein continued to be an avid reader, recalling that even during this period she "read as much as the housework would permit."[10] However, the inner academic beckoned Edith again before too long, and Stein returned to school in 1908, preparing rigorously with a half-year of private tutoring for her entrance examination to the *Obersekunda*.

Back at home, Stein continued to grow interiorly and intellectually within her enchanted literary world:

> I used (my free time) principally for reading, preferably drama: Grillparzer, Hebbel, Ibsen, and, above all, Shakespeare became my daily bread. I was much more at home in this colorful world of the great passions and deeds than in the everyday life around me.[11]

Upon her return to school, Stein's academic courses nourished her literary soul with formative depth from her friends, the poets:

> In Schiller's philosophical poems, I found a world-view that suited me. Our regular curriculum closed with the Classic poets. But as a generous supplement, we were given an overview of the dramatic poetry of the nineteenth century. Grillparzer, Hebbel, Otto Ludwig: these, after all, were intimate friends of mine.[12]

Alongside her enjoyment of the literary arts, Stein's ready response to the visual arts is apparent from a young age. The

Stein family lived in a gracious home, in a city of cultural offerings. This exposure to beauty was deeply appreciated and internalized by the young art lover. On one occasion, during grade school, Stein precociously recommended a reproduction of Swiss painter Arnold Böcklin's *Töteninsel* as a farewell gift for a beloved professor:

> The picture: towering trees in the center of an impression of vibrant but somber life as contrast to the unexpected light on the cliff which seems to instill hope into an otherwise dismal scene. A skiff transporting a garlanded stone coffin to the *Island of the Dead* is, with its rower, more naturally lighted than the brilliantly lit main figure standing immobile, facing the coffin and the island.
>
> It may seem a remarkable choice for a thirteen-year-old student to make; however, Böcklin's works were on display in the Silesian Museum in Breslau, and there was an Academy of Art, as well.
>
> Edith's appreciation of art is demonstrated by her frequent allusions to the works of famous artists, reproductions of which graced the homes of teachers and friends.[13]

Stein's aesthetic eye also rejoiced in the beauty of the natural world. She loved the outdoors and especially enjoyed long hikes in the surrounding countryside well into her university years. With the eye of an artist, she seamlessly relates the natural beauty to depictions in the visual arts, drawing a ready parallel to an artistic rendition of a similar setting during one of her many hiking excursions:

> When we looked down into the valley from that height, I had such a feeling of being in the heart of Germany: a lovely landscape on the slopes, carefully husbanded fields, neat villages, and an encircling wreath of green forests. It seemed as though the very next moment one might expect a wedding procession to emerge from the woods on the opposite hill, just as Ludwig Richter depicted in one of his paintings.[14]

Furthermore, Stein consistently turned to artistic expression as a natural outlet for her astute mental powers. Time and again in family and school settings Stein offered her services as poet and playwright, producing a bright array of compositions for the celebration of special occasions including birthdays and weddings, school excursions and commencement day. One occasional piece which Stein composed in her youth, and which she recounts in detail in her autobiography, was a dramatic sketch enacted by the students in Stein's class for their high school graduation celebration:

> I was given the coveted task of writing the Bier-drama (beer-skit) during this time. I did not keep a copy of it but I can still remember the plot. The heroine was a graduate who had just completed her examinations. All the studying has completely confused her spirit, and her mother takes her to a magician who is to expel the evil spirits. He conjures them up and they appear, one after the other: Cicero, Horace, Frau von Stein, Gretchen, Klärchen, etc. Finally, the patient awakens as from a bad dream; she feels well but has not a shred of knowledge left. Then she finds a paper which dispels every one of her cares:
> Though there's no knowledge in my head
> I fear no one; nothing I dread
> This paper states in clearest type
> For the university I'm ripe.
> ... The beer-skit had given me great concern because even at dress-rehearsal time the actresses had not full command of their parts. But, naturally, all went well by the time of the performance. I was not one of the actors but, rather, the director and prompter. At its conclusion, the author was called for and, at center stage, "Horace" crowned me with his wreath.[15]

This artistic tie with family celebrations remained unchanged, even as Stein matured and her academic work removed her from the daily familial circle. "My participation at birthday parties and other family feasts was never curtailed," she recalls, "and it remained my responsibility to provide the necessary poetry."[16] Stein's sister Erna also notes this characteristic artistic contribution:

> When in 1920, I married my college friend Hans Biberstein, Edith, of course, was present at the wedding. She composed delightful poems for all the nieces and nephews, in which she recalled the most enjoyable events of our student years and childhood.[17]

A short play which Stein wrote for her sister's wedding reception festivities has been passed down in family memory. The witty plot of the skit is lovingly described here by Erna's daughter, Susanne Batzdorff:

> Wolf (Batzdorff's cousin) also remembers how he and his cousins, Gerhard and Erika, participated in a playlet which their aunt Edith had written as entertainment for my parents' wedding celebration in December 1920. Gerhard played the stork, who was attempting to persuade two young babies, one male and one female, to accompany him to the newlyweds, Hans and Erna Biberstein, to be their children. The amusing question-and-answer repartee entered into family legend.[18]

The enthusiasm for the arts which blossomed in Stein's early years continued to deepen as she matured. Her artistic focus, however, broadens as she steps into the realm of faith. A new vista opens before her, and the arts do not disappoint. Throughout her adulthood and conversion years, as well as at the culmination of her journey in faith, the arts will remain for Stein a constant companion and guide.

Adulthood and Conversion

Stein embarked upon her University career in literature, philosophy, and history, just two years after Prussian universities began admitting women. Both the prudence and practicality of such a decision met with resistance within her extensive family circle. It was ultimately her mother, Frau Stein, who stood unwaveringly behind Stein's academic aspirations and played a decisive role in supporting what was considered a controversial vocational decision:

> No one interfered with my choice of profession. My mother's protecting hand shielded it ... She wanted me to have full freedom of choice.
> "No one has a right to tell you what to do. After all, no one's making us a contribution toward it. Do whatever you think is right for you."
> So, without a care, I was able to pursue my goal.[19]

Frau Stein's support at this important juncture is fundamental to Stein's vocational path. Stein's mother has proven herself more than once in offering such affirmation. We learn of another occasion in which Frau Stein supported a relative's aspirations to a career in the dramatic arts:

> So it was that she championed her young brother-in-law Leo when he "disgraced" his mother by aspiring to be an actor. She took him into her own home when his mother would no longer tolerate him in hers; and, when she heard him get up during the night to recite his lines, she was so convinced that his calling was genuine that she sought to mediate between him and Grandmother. (Later as Leo Walter Stein he became well known as a playwright of comedies and as a stage director. Because of their nationalistic content, some of his theater pieces, "The King's Ballerina," and "Liselotte von der Pfalz," were even deemed worthy of presentation on the German stage of the Third Reich.)[20]

Enabled with her mother's support to pursue her academic interests, Stein began in Breslau the studies which would lead her to Göttingen, Freiburg, and beyond, as her pursuit of the truth, both in philosophy and faith, became her life's vocation and focus. For her State Board examination at the end of her university studies, Stein underwent a rigorous "stroll" from Livy and Plato through the Middle High German epics, folk literature, Faust, and Romanticism, with great agility.[21] Passing the daunting exams with highest honors, Stein received from her impressed examiners one conclusive remark, "The lady is well informed in general."[22]

These final examinations mark the turning point in Stein's academic career to a full-time concentration in philosophy. She will eventually pursue her doctoral dissertation under the guidance of leading phenomenologist Edmund Husserl. Known as the "Father of Phenomenology," Husserl discussed with Stein the possibility of pursuing a doctorate in either history or literature. But Stein's decision was firm: "I want to prove to myself whether I am capable of an independent achievement in philosophy."[23]

One of the most compelling dramas written by Stein during her academic career, in fact, depicts a philosophical encounter between Edmund Husserl and St. Thomas Aquinas. Stein had been invited to submit a contribution to a special commemorative issue of the *Jahrbuch für Philosophie und phänomenologische Forshung* in honor of Edmund Husserl's seventieth birthday. She wishes to submit a comparison between the tenets of Husserl's phenomenology and the philosophy of St. Thomas Aquinas. What better way to present this comparison than to have the character of St. Thomas appear as a guest at Husserl's birthday party? St. Thomas arrives just as the birthday celebrations are ending. Husserl invites the venerable thinker to draw up a chair, and the two amicably discuss their approaches to the search for truth.

When Stein submitted her imaginary dialogue to the *Jahrbuch* for publication, the editor of the edition, Martin Heidegger, turned down the play, "asking for a more 'neutral' treatment of the subject matter."[24] Stein rewrites her piece in essay form for publication in the 1929 *Festschrift*. Her original presentation, however, with its *dramatis personae* and simple stage directions, reveals Stein's instinctive mode of expression in artistic form to convey the philosophical dialogue unfolding within her mind.

Her dramatic skit, entitled, "What is Philosophy? A Conversation between Edmund Husserl and Thomas Aquinas," was eventually published alongside its revised academic version "An Attempt to Contrast Husserl's Phenomenology and the Philosophy of St. Thomas Aquinas," in *Knowledge and Faith*. With wit and lucidity, Stein's fictional dialogue highlights her creative gifts:

> **Husserl** (*alone*): My good visitors meant well with their kind birthday wishes and I certainly would not have missed a one. But after such a day it is hard to relax, and I have always been one for a good night's sleep. Actually, after all the chatter I would appreciate a decent conversation on philosophy to get my mind on track.
> (*A knock*) At this late hour? Come in, please.
> **A Religious** (*in white habit and black mantle*): I'm sorry to bother you so late at night, Professor, but I heard what you just said and thought I might still chance a visit. I wanted to speak with you today—just you and I, for I do not take part in social gatherings—but since early morning I have not had the chance to be alone with you until now.
> **Husserl** (*kindly but somewhat at a loss*): You are most welcome, Reverend Father. I've had religious as students before, but to tell the truth I don't remember having any with your particular color-scheme. Could you please help out my poor memory?
> **The priest** (*smiling slightly*): No, I have never sat at your feet. Only from afar have I followed with great interest how your philosophy arose and evolved. And some of your students have come and told me about you. I am Thomas Aquinas.
> **Husserl**: Well, this is certainly the biggest surprise of the day. Do sit down. Forgive me if I am unsure how I should act. I would be grateful for some advice.
> **Thomas**: Quite casually, please. Treat me like any other visitor who comes to talk about philosophy. That's why I'm here, you see.

> **Husserl**: Then do come and sit over here in the corner of my old leather sofa. I've had it ever since I first lectured at the university, but it's quite comfortable and I doubt I'll ever part with it. May I sit right here by you in my old armchair? And now we can begin our discussion. What sort of topic do you have in mind?[25]

Stein also nourished a passionate love of music and theater through the many cultural offerings of her university years. Theater lovers can identify with Stein's eager anticipation of a dramatic performance:

> Even more than reading, I enjoyed going to the theater. During those years, every time the presentation of a classical drama was announced, it was as though I had been tendered a personal invitation. An anticipated evening at the theater was like a brilliant star which gradually drew nearer. I counted the intervening days and hours. It was a great delight just to sit in the theater and wait for the heavy iron curtain to be raised slowly; the call bell finally sounded; and the new unknown world was revealed. Then I became totally immersed in the happenings on the stage, and the humdrum of everyday disappeared.[26]

Along with her love of theatrical works, Stein's enthusiastic interest for operatic and classical music also deepens in these years. She loves the regularity of the music of Bach and will eventually discover her musical home in the world of Gregorian chant:

> I loved the classical operas as much as I did the great tragedies. The first I heard was *The Magic Flute*. We bought the piano score and soon knew it by heart. So, too, with *Fidelio* which always remained my favorite. I also heard Wagner and during a performance found it impossible wholly to evade its magic. Still I repudiated this music, with the sole exception of *Die Meistersinger*. I had a predilection for Bach. This world of purity and strict regularity attracted me most intimately. Later when I came to know Gregorian

chant, I felt completely at home for the first time; and then I understood what had moved me so much in Bach.²⁷

The large extended Stein family also treasured Aunt Edith's storytelling ability. Her young nieces and nephews would sit on the floor in rapt attention at the tales their beloved aunt would weave. "During our aunt's annual visits, we children especially looked forward to her story hours, when she would gather us around her and read us from some of her favorite tales, which were to become our favorites, too."²⁸ Stein's niece, Suzanne, describes those enthralling stories:

> I remember especially the adventures of Nonny and Manny, two young boys in Iceland, who had the most exciting seafaring adventures. The author, Jan Svensson, was a consummate storyteller, who spun his yarns with spellbinding excitement and suspense that kept all of us on the edge of our seats. When I discovered that my aunt knew the author personally, I asked her to help me write him a letter to let him know how much we had enjoyed his books. Some weeks later, I was thrilled to receive a reply from him, probably my first letter from a published author.²⁹

This niece was not the only little person upon whom Stein's story hours would make an impression. In 1983, fifty years after last seeing Stein, her nephew Ernst Ludwig Biberstein recounted:

> She was something like the good fairy in one of those fairy tales which she would tell or read to us when she came to Breslau for a visit ... Tante Edith was part of a different world. Why was that? She was not the only one of her siblings who only appeared for a few weeks per year ... For me it was first of all the fact that Tante Edith came from an area which I only knew from the field of saga and the romance of ballads and equated it with those. That's where she was "at home," in the geographic as well as allegorical sense.³⁰

Stein's niece Lotte Sachs also recalled of Aunt Edith, "I ... remember with pleasure us children sitting in a semicircle around her on the floor while she either told us stories or read to us; back in my mind they were stories about Iceland or Norway."³¹ This same niece was given a literary present by Stein at a decisive moment in the young girl's life. Before emigrating to America due to the Nazi persecution, Lotte made a final stop to visit Tante Edith at the Carmel of Cologne. As a parting gift in these harrowing circumstances, Stein gave her niece a novella by Norwegian author Bjørnstjerne Bjørnssen:

> It is inscribed, in German, "To dear Lotte, as a memento of her visit to Carmel." It was neither a religious tract, nor a missionary text designed to influence Lotte to turn toward Christianity, but a novella by Bjørnssen. That fascinated me, for my mother's bookcase contained a complete set of Bjørnssen's works, and as a teenager I read many of his stories. I guess he must have been a favorite of Aunt Edith as well.³²

Stein's choice of such a gift for her young niece, who was "eighteen at the time, traveling alone and toward an uncertain future,"³³ reinforces our understanding of Stein's deep appreciation of literature. She continues a connection with a beloved niece, exiled from family and country by the Nazi regime, through their shared love of literature.

The arts will also accompany Stein through profound inner transformations. During her university years in Göttingen, Stein was discovering the realm of faith for the first time. Her perceptions were changing, and a new world was unfolding before her. As her inner life opens to the spiritual fullness of the Christian vision, Stein's beloved artistic realm greets her anew.

One new encounter with faith through art occurs for Stein during a visit to the Liebig Institute in Frankfurt. Stein is on a cultural visit with her good friend, Pauline Reinach, the sister of Stein's favorite professor, Adolf Reinach. As the two young women toured the museum, Stein's artistic vista expands:

> Pauline led me along the River Main to the Liebig Institute where Myrion's *Athene* stands. But before we

reached that statue we passed through a room where a sculptured group taken from a Flemish grave of the sixteenth century was displayed: the Mother of God, and John, in the center; Magdalen and Nicodemus on either side. There was no longer an image of Christ in the group. These figures had such an overpowering effect on us that, for a long while, we were unable to tear ourselves away. And as we went on from there to see the Athene, I found her very attractive but she left me cold. Only when I paid another visit there many years later was I able to appreciate her.[34]

Sr. M. Amata Neyer, OCD, curator of the Edith-Stein-Archiv, in Cologne, discussed this moment in Stein's artistic and personal journey, astutely observing:

> Stein never intended to be so overpowered by the Flemish group. Indeed, she had not even gone to the Institute to see it. Her interest as an aesthete was purely in the Athene. Yet, she was transfixed, literally incapable of moving on from this scene, and the impression which it left upon her was significant.[35]

Stein encounters Christ and the Christian faith through the sculptural depiction of the mourners at Christ's tomb. The moving compassion depicted in the figures touches Stein's soul. This artistic encounter marks a defining moment in Stein's journey of conversion, as her soul opens to the transformative influence of faith. Believing Christians who cross Stein's path, presenting the faith to her in living form, will be the decisive element of her conversion. Their personal witness of Christ will so impact Stein's journey of faith that she calls these individuals "living images (*lebendige Bilder*)," which, she asserts, speak to us "even better than those of wood or stone."[36]

Faith and Carmel

In God's perfect faithfulness, the arts greet Stein anew as she enters the Catholic faith and ultimately seeks His Will behind the grille of the Carmelite cloister. One artistic relationship, which Stein forms in the years immediately following her conversion to Catholicism, is her friendship with celebrated Catholic authoress, and fellow convert, Gertrud von le Fort.

These two remarkable women first met in Munich during Easter Week of 1932. They established a deep friendship which vigorously continued even after Stein withdrew behind the enclosure of Carmel. The depth of their relationship is evidenced in a letter which Stein wrote to von le Fort shortly before entering the Carmelite Order. Stein expresses her struggle with her mother Frau Stein's lack of understanding for both her conversion and, an even deeper blow to her mother, Stein's decision to enter a cloistered religious order:

> Your dear letter made me very happy. It is so good for me during these very difficult last days (at home) to receive something from people who understand my path—in contrast to the great pain I must be causing here and have before my eyes daily. You will help me, won't you, to beg that my mother will be given the strength to bear the leave-taking and the light to understand it? I have often thought it would mean a great deal to you to know my mother. She has a certain resemblance to Veronica's grandmother, only she is not a person of culture, but rather of a very simple and strong nature.[37]

Ever conversant with literary figures, Stein references "Veronica's grandmother," a character from Gertrud von le Fort's novel *Das Schweisstuch der Veronika* (*Veronica's Veil*), as a fitting image of Stein's own mother. Frau Stein's inability to understand Stein's conversion, or to support her decision to enter a cloistered religious order, is a deep suffering for Stein. In fact,

Frau Stein will painfully cut off all communication with Stein for years after Stein's entrance into the cloister of Carmel.

Notwithstanding this blow to their relationship, Stein continues to write to her mother weekly and prays for her mother to be given interior light. In this regard, we learn of a miracle which occurred at the moment of Frau Stein's death. Stein, now Sr. Teresa Benedicta of the Cross, was renewing her vows on the Feast of the Exaltation of the Holy Cross, September 14, 1936. At the very moment of the renewal of vows, she receives a deep interior intuition regarding her mother:

> Afterward she said to one of her sisters who was specially intimate with her, "*When it was my turn to renew my vows my mother was beside me. I felt her presence quite distinctly.*" On that same day a telegram came from Breslau with the news that Frau Stein had died—at the very time when her daughter was renewing her vows.[38]

Another interesting correlation exists between Stein and her literary friend's best-known work, *The Song at the Scaffold*. Von le Fort was researching this historical novel, depicting the execution of Carmelite religious during the French Revolution, in the period when she met Stein. In a letter to a fellow religious sister, Stein explains:

> You have asked me twice, I believe, whether I have any connection to Gertrud von le Fort's Carmelite novella *Die Letzte am Schafott* (*The Song at the Scaffold*, trans. Olga Marx (New York, NY: Sheed & Ward, 1933). She hit upon the material without my having anything to do with it. However, soon thereafter she came to see me in Munich, and one afternoon we spoke about Carmel, from which she was spiritually still rather distant at that time. She only became engrossed in it through her work on the novella. Naturally she has also visited us when she was here (in Cologne) and was very happy to have the two hours at the grate. [39]

An article written by Stein during her Carmelite years, which appeared in the Sunday supplement of the *Ausburger Postzeitung* on 31 March 1935, expresses her appreciation for von le Fort's contribution to Carmel through this novel and other works:

> Until a few years ago, very little from our silent monasteries penetrated into the world. It is different today. People talk a lot about Carmel and want to hear something about life behind the high walls ... Gertrud von le Fort's novel about Carmel has vigorously directed German intellectual circles to our Order, as has her beautiful foreword to the letters of Marie Antoinette de Geuser.[40]

Fittingly, Stein's first visitor in her new life as a Carmelite religious in Cologne was an artist. We learn this detail from a letter written by Stein to her philosopher friend and godmother, Hedwig Conrad-Martius, shortly after entering Carmel. "Actually, during the postulancy one ought not to have visitors," Stein notes. "But a few have been here just the same. The first one was Pater Petrus from Neuburg Abbey, whom we visited together last year (the painter, not the philosopher)."[41]

A first visit from an artist to Stein behind the grille of Carmel is also fitting in another sense. As Stein's contemplative soul reaches its home in Carmel, her artistic sensibility finds its welcome here as well. Carmelite spirituality has a longstanding tradition of celebration through the arts. The Carmel tradition celebrates feast days and holidays with dramatic productions, recitations, and musical performances. One may recall the photograph of St. Thérèse of Lisieux dressed as St. Joan of Arc for one of the dramas produced in her Carmel of Lisieux. Furthermore, the great Carmelite co-reformer, St. John of the Cross, was a mystical poet, a visual artist, and a craftsman.

Stein's letters provide a glimpse into her celebration through the arts in keeping with this Carmelite tradition. She participated in these in-house theatricals with enthusiasm, and the celebration of Stein's own 50th birthday in 1941 is no exception. She details the dramatic performance for the occasion:

> Just think, Your Reverence—I saw not only Abraham, but Enoch and Noah as well, Isaac and Jacob, Moses and

Aaron, David, Elijah and Elisha. They all appeared just as they are described in the Book of Ecclesiasticus (Sirach 44–48). Abraham was a most distinguished personage (Mother Subprioress). As for Moses, only his nose was impressive; the rest of him was small and quaint; the reverse of his Tablet of the Commandments was seen to be last week's kitchen list (Sister Agatha).[42]

In a letter to her friend Mother Petra Brüning, of the Ursuline Sisters in Dorsten, Stein reveals preparations for another theatrical production:

> Many thanks also for the generous provision of dramatic literature. We want to put on part of *Metanoeite* for the profession of our Sister Baptista, probably on the (feast of) the Visitation. She has a great devotion to (John) the Baptizer, so at the end of the play she will receive the book itself.[43]

Stein also recounts her own participation in such dramatic productions. "On the 28th, you would even have gotten to see me as St. Francis,"[44] she reveals, describing a play presented by the novitiate in Cologne for the Feast of the Holy Innocents in December, 1934.

Even during the difficulties and dangers of wartime conditions, this Carmelite artistic tradition continued uninterrupted. After the horror of Kristallnacht in 1938, Stein is transferred for safety to the Carmel of Echt, in the Netherlands. She is soon taking part in artistic celebrations with her new community. In a letter sent shortly after her transfer, Stein references "the brief play on the Sacraments that opened the nameday celebration on Thursday evening."[45]

Stein not only enjoyed these dramatic productions as a spectator and player; she often supplied the scripts through her own original compositions. "Edith ... was artistically inclined", biographer Freda Mary Oben affirms. "She loved plastic art, sculpture, paintings and music. She kept small cards depicting famous paintings. Near the Madonna, she kept a silver vase made in Japan. She wrote poems and little plays."[46] Unfortunately, the poems and plays which Stein wrote during her years in Cologne were "all burned when the convent was bombed in 1944."[47] The spiritual poems and dramatic dialogues written by Stein after her transfer to Echt have, fortunately, survived. These works, overflowing with mystical insight and passionate faith, comprise some of Stein's most intimate offerings of artistic expression and self-revelation.

A moving example is offered in the poetic dialogue "Conversation at Night," written by Stein for the birthday celebration of Mother Antonia, 13 June 1941. In this dramatic work, Stein depicts a nighttime encounter between the Echt prioress and the Old Testament figure Queen Esther. Stein reveals her own identification with Esther, whose profound concern for the sufferings of her Jewish people compelled her supplication before her husband King Ahasuerus for their salvation. Stein herself is now pleading spiritually for her Jewish people before the Heavenly Throne of Christ, her King. The persecution of her own family and the Jewish people under the heavy hand of National Socialism has united Stein with Queen Esther in a personal and vocational sense:

> If only they knew where to go! But I trust that, from eternity, Mother will take care of them. And (I also trust) in the Lord's having accepted my life for all of them. I keep having to think of Queen Esther who was taken from among her people precisely that she might represent them before the king. I am a very poor and powerless little Esther, but the King who chose me is infinitely great and merciful. That is a great comfort.[48]

Edith presents the suffering through Esther's eyes, and Esther intercedes again for the Jewish people as "another Haman" swears to annihilate them:

> Esther:
> It was hard indeed.
> Yet it was God's will, and I remained
> The poor maidservant of the Lord at the king's palace.
> My faithful uncle followed after me.

He often came to the palace's door and brought news
Of our people's needs and danger.
So there came the day when I approached the king
To plead for rescue from the deadly enemy.
Life or death hung on his gaze.
I leaned on the shoulders of my maid.
But I was not alarmed before my husband's wrath.
The eye that met mine was entirely friendly.
In full favor, he handed me the scepter.
Then my spirit was borne out of time and place.
High in the clouds there was another throne,
On which sits the Lord of Lords, before whom pales
The earthly lord's vain glory.
He himself, the Eternal, bowed down
And promised me the salvation of my people.
I sank down before the throne of the Highest as though dead.
I found myself again in the arms of my husband.
He addressed me lovingly and said that any wish—
Whatever it might be—he would grant to me.
This is how the highest Lord freed his people
Through Esther, his maidservant, from the hands of Haman.

Mother:
And today another Haman
Has sworn to annihilate them in bitter hate.
Is this in fact why Esther has returned?[49]

In this spiritual drama, the Queen of Carmel has sent Esther to invoke the intercession of these prayerful, cloistered souls for the sufferings of Her people in the present darkness:

Esther:
You're the one who says so—
Yes, I am traveling through the world
To plead for lodgings for the homeless,
The people so scattered and trampled
That still cannot die.
… The people are in confusion and cannot find rest,
An object of disdain and scorn:

> It will be thus until the final battle.
> But before the cross appears again in heaven,
> Even before Elijah comes to gather his own,
> The good Shepherd goes silently through the lands.
> Now and then he gathers from the depths of the abyss
> A little lamb, shelters it at his heart.
> And then others always follow him.
> But there above at the throne of grace
> The Mother ceaselessly pleads for her people.
> She seeks souls to help her pray.
> Then only when Israel has found the Lord,
> Only then when He has received His own,
> Will He come in manifest glory.
> And we must pray for this second coming.
>
> Mother:
> Like once the first—I understand exactly.
> You were the pathfinder for the first coming,
> Now you are clearing the way to the kingdom of glory.
> You came to me—do I now understand the message?
> The Queen of Carmel sent you.
> Where else was she to find hearts prepared
> If not in her quiet sanctuary?
> Her people, which are yours: your Israel,
> I'll take it up into the lodgings of my heart.
> Praying secretly and sacrificing secretly,
> I'll take it home to my Savior's heart.[50]

Esther then reveals the redemptive effect of Christ's sacrifice on the Cross, as experienced by those who awaited His coming in the bosom of Abraham:

> Esther:
> Like all who faithfully have served the Lord
> As their ancestors did. We waited there in peace,
> Still far from the light, so always in longing.
> But there came a day when, through all of creation,
> There occurred a fissure. All the elements seemed
> To be in revolt, night enveloped

> The world at noon. But in the midst of the night
> There stood, as if illumined by lightning, a barren mountain,
> And on the mountain a cross on which someone hung
> Bleeding from a thousand wounds; a thirst came over us
> To drink ourselves well from this fountain of wounds.
> The cross vanished into night, yet our night
> Was suddenly penetrated by a new light,
> Of which we had never had any idea: a sweet, blessed light.
> It streamed from the wounds of that man
> Who had just died on the cross; now he stood
> In our midst. He himself was the light,
> The eternal light, that we had longed for from of old,
> The Father's reflection and the salvation of the people.
> He spread his arms wide and spoke
> With a voice full of heavenly timbre:
> Come to me all you who have faithfully served
> The Father and lived in hope
> Of the Redeemer; see, He is with you,
> He fetches you home to his Father's kingdom.
> What happened then, there are no words to describe.
> All of us who had awaited blessedness,
> We were now at our goal—in the heart of Jesus.[51]

The Old Testament figure of Queen Esther appears once again in the moving texts Stein chooses for her *Missa et Officium in Honorem B.V.M. Reginae Pacis*, composed in Carmel at the request of her religious superiors and submitted to the Vatican for the approval of a Feast for Carmel in Mary's honor under the title Queen of Peace. The texts never received the approval sought by the Order.[52] Stein discusses this liturgical endeavor in her letters of March and April 1940, noting:

> During Lent, (my mind) was allowed to do something very nice: to compose a Mass and Office in honor of the Blessed Virgin Mary, *Regina Pacis* (Queen of Peace) for the Carmel of Cologne, which wishes to ask Rome for a First Class Feast, preferably for the whole Church, but at least for the whole Order. The Picpus Fathers and Sisters already have such a feast, so do our Fathers of the Flemish Province,

whose patroness is the *Regina Pacis*; but they use the Common of Our Lady for nearly everything. Now that we have all the parts proper except the Psalms and the hymns of the Little Hours, we have only to await Rome's reply.[53]

It is noteworthy that along with other Scriptural sources, Stein draws from the Book of Esther for this compilation of spiritual reading and liturgical prayer. She chooses The Book of Esther, Chapter Seven, verses 1–4, for the Second Reading of the Office, which includes Queen Esther's plea to the King:

> And on the second day, as they were drinking wine, the king again said to Esther, "What is your petition, Queen Esther? It shall be granted you. And what is your request? Even to half of my kingdom, it shall be fulfilled." Then Queen Esther answered, "If I have found favor in your sight, O King, and if it please the king, let my life be given me at my petition, and my people at my request. For we are sold, I and my people, to be destroyed, to be slain, and to be annihilated."[54]

Esther's voice then sings through the Third Reading of the Office, in praise of the God who keeps His faithfulness to His people. "And my nation, this is Israel, who cried out to God and were saved. The Lord has saved his people; the Lord has delivered us from all these evils; God has delivered us from all these evils; God has done great signs and wonders, which have not occurred among the nations."[55] Stein confirms her "unshakable hope"[56] in the salvific power of Her Savior through the ultimate surrender of her life to the Lord's Holy and Inscrutable Will. Encouraging her sister with the words "Come, let us go for our people,"[57] Stein will offer her life with the faith and trust of Queen Esther for their salvation.

Notes

1. Edith Stein, *Life in a Jewish Family*, trans. Josephine Koeppel, OCD, ed Dr. L. Gelber and Romaeus Leuven, *The Collected Works of Edith Stein*, Vol. 1 (Washington, DC: ICS Publications, 1986) 171.
2. Stein, *Life*, 170.
3. Stein, *Life*, 77–78.
4. Stein, *Life*, 47.
5. Jean de Fabrégues, *Edith Stein: Philospher, Carmelite Nun, Holocaust Martyr* (Boston: St. Paul Books and Media, 1993) 12.
6. Dr. Erna Biberstein, from "Reminiscences" in Editor's Foreword to *Life*, 14.
7. Stein, *Life*, 63, 78.
8. Stein, *Life*, 71–72
9. Stein, *Life*, 145, 138.
10. Stein, *Life*, 148.
11. Stein, *Life*, 150.
12. Stein, *Life*, 170.
13. Josephine Koeppel, OCD, explanatory note 32 to Stein, *Life*, 475–6. (Artistic Reference: Arnold Böcklin, Swiss Painter, 1827–1901, *Island of the Dead*, 1880, Kunstmuseum, Basel).
14. Stein, *Life*, 244. (Artistic Reference: Ludwig Richter, German Romantic Artist, 1803–1884, *The Bridal Procession*, 1847, Dresden Gallery).
15. Stein, *Life*, 175, 178.
16. Stein, *Life*, 215.
17. Erna Biberstein, née Stein. "Reminiscences," from the Editor's Foreword, in Stein, *Life*, 17.
18. Susanne M. Batzdorff, *Aunt Edith: The Jewish Heritage of a Catholic Saint* (Springfield: Templegate Publishers, 1998) 121.
19. Stein, *Life*, 173.
20. Stein, *Life*, 38–39.
21. Stein, *Life*, 313.
22. Stein, *Life*, 314.
23. Stein, *Life*, 317.
24. Steven Payne, OCD, "Foreword to the ICS Edition," in *Knowledge and Faith*, trans. Walter Redmond, ed. Dr. L. Gelber and Michael Linssen,

OCD, *The Collected Works of Edith Stein*, Vol. 8, (Washington, DC: ICS Publications, 2000) xi-xii.
25. Edith Stein, "What is Philosophy? A Conversation Between Edmund Husserl and Thomas Aquinas" from "Husserl and Aquinas: A Comparison," in *Knowledge and Faith*, 2-3.
26. Stein, *Life*, 171-2.
27. Stein, *Life*, 172.
28. Batzdorff, *Aunt Edith*, 125.
29. Batzdorff, *Aunt Edith*, 125.
30. Biberstein, Ernst Ludwig, "Erinnerungen an Edith Stein," in Herbstrith, Waltraud, ed.: *Edith Stein, eine grosse Glaubenszeugin*, Plöger, 1986, p. 130-131. (Translation by Batzdorff, in *Aunt Edith*, 119-120).
31. Lotte Stein Sachs, from Letter dated November 10, 1997, p. 2, in Batzdorff, *Aunt Edith*, 126.
32. Batzdorff, *Aunt Edith*, 227 note 14, 128.
33. Batzdorff, *Aunt Edith*, 227 note 14, 127.
34. Stein, *Life*, 401. (Artistic References: Myron, Greek Sculptor. 5th Century B.C., *Athene*, 460 B.C., Roman Copy, Vatican Museum, and *Flemish Burial Scene*, 16th Century, Liebieghaus Skulpturensammlung, Frankfurt am Main).
35. Sr. M. Amata Neyer, OCD, Edith-Stein-Archiv, Karmel "Maria vom Frieden," Cologne, Germany, Interview with author, 8 March 2002.
36. Edith Stein, *The Science of the Cross: A Study of St. John of the Cross*, trans. Hilda Graef, ed. Dr. L. Gelber and Romaeus Leuven, OCD, (London: Burns and Oates, 1960) 209, (pg. 276 in ICS Publications edition).
37. Edith Stein, *Self-Portrait in Letters 1916-1942*, trans. Josephine Koeppel, O.C.D, ed. Dr. L. Gelber and Romaeus Leuven, OCD, The Collected Works of Edith Stein, Vol. 5, (Washington, DC: ICS Publications, 1993) Letter 156, to Gertrud von le Fort.
38. Posselt, *Edith Stein*, 167, italics given. Posselt notes the following: "Confirmation of the simultaneity in time-frame is given in both Letter 239 and 262, *Self-Portrait in Letters*, pg. 251 and pg. 275."
39. Stein, *Self-Portrait in Letters*, Letter 196, to Mother Petra Brüning, OSU.
40. Stein, "On the History and Spirit of Carmel," *The Hidden Life*, 1.
41. Stein, *Self-Portrait in Letters*, Letter 160. For additional references by Stein, see *Self-Portrait in Letters*, Letters 104, 164, and 202. The artist's secular name is Anton Jans (b. Kressbach, 1887, d. Neersdomer Mühle, 1970).
42. Stein, *Self-Portrait in Letters*, Letter 324, to Mother Johanna van Weersth,

OCD.
43. Stein, *Self-Portrait in Letters*, Letter 219, to Mother Petra Brüning, OSU.
44. Stein, *Self-Portrait in Letters*, Letter 190, to Ruth Kantorowicz.
45. Stein, *Self-Portrait in Letters*, Letter 321, to Mother Petra Brüning, OSU.
46. Freda Mary Oben, *The Life and Thought of St. Edith Stein*, (New York: Alba House, 2001) 49. (Artistic Reference: Desiderius Lenz, OSB, 1832–1928, *Mother of Life*, Beuron School of Art, Edith-Stein-Archiv, Karmel Maria vom Frieden, Cologne).
47. Oben, *Life and Thought*, 49.
48. Stein, *Self-Portrait in Letters*, Letter 281, to Mother Petra Brüning, OSU.
49. Stein, "Conversation at Night," *The Hidden Life*, 130–1.
50. Stein, "Conversation at Night," *The Hidden Life*, 131–3.
51. Stein, "Conversation at Night," *The Hidden Life*, 131–2.
52. See Appendix. *Missa et Officium in Honorem B.V.M. Reginae Pacis*, Edith-Stein-Archiv, Karmel "Maria vom Frieden," Cologne, Germany, published in Elizabeth A. Mitchell, *Artist and Image: Artistic Creativity and Personal Formation in the Thought of Edith Stein* (Memphis: St. Paul Institute, 2021) https://stpaulmemphis.com/product/the-artist-the-image/.
53. Stein, *Self-Portrait in Letters*, Letter 311, to Sr. Agnella Stadtmüller, OP.
54. Esther 7:1–4, as quoted in *Missa et Officium in Honorem B.V.M. Reginae Pacis*, Edith-Stein-Archiv, Karmel "Maria vom Frieden," Cologne, Germany, published in Elizabeth A. Mitchell, *Artist and Image: Artistic Creativity and Personal Formation in the Thought of Edith Stein* (Memphis: St. Paul Institute, 2021) https://stpaulmemphis.com/product/the-artist-the-image/.
55. Esther 10:9, as quoted in *Missa et Officium in Honorem B.V.M. Reginae Pacis*, Edith-Stein-Archiv, Karmel "Maria vom Frieden," Cologne, Germany, published in Elizabeth A. Mitchell, *Artist and Image: Artistic Creativity and Personal Formation in the Thought of Edith Stein* (Memphis: St. Paul Institute, 2021) https://stpaulmemphis.com/product/the-artist-the-image/.
56. *Positio Super Martyrio et Super Virtutibus Canonizationis Servae Dei Teresiae Benedictae a Cruce* (Tipografia Guerra, Roma: 1986) "Relatio," 66, translation mine.
57. As quoted in Sr. Maria Amata Neyer, OCD, *Edith Stein: Her Life in Photos and Documents*, trans. Waltraut Stein, Ph.D. (Washington, DC: ICS Publications, 1999) 74.

2 THE LIVING IMAGE

> *Behind all things of value to be found in this world stands the person of the Creator who, as prefigurement, encloses all earthly values in Himself and transmits them.*
>
> Stein, *Essays on Woman*[1]

The arts are a treasure which Stein has appreciated for their formative influence in her own life and to which she instinctively turns to express her deepest thoughts and experiences. Beyond the fashioning of an artwork by the artist, lies the fashioning of the human being by the Hand of the Divine Artist, the Creator, whose artistic masterpiece is the human person. Our encounter with an individual whose life is a fulfillment of the divine design intended by the Hand of God affects us as profoundly as an artistic masterpiece. We are moved even more deeply by the living image, in fact, because the material which speaks to us is the human soul, fashioned by grace.

The Image Stirs

Stein addresses the interplay between the Divine Artist and the human person in a dramatic dialogue she composed in the Carmel of Echt in 1939. This dialogue, entitled "I Am Always in Your Midst," presents an encounter between St. Angela Merici and an Ursuline religious. Stein composed their imagined conversation as a stage play to be performed in Carmel by the novices for the name-day celebration of the convent Mother Superior. Through the character of Mother Ursula, Stein details the formative work of the Lord as the master craftsman of our soul, describing us as God's work of art:

> Of course, the Lord leads each on her own path,
> And what we call "fate" is the artist's doing,
> The eternal Artist, who creates material for himself
> And forms it into images in various ways:
> By gentle finger strokes and also by chisel blows.
> But he does not work on dead material;
> His greatest creative joy in fact is
> That under his hand the image stirs,
> That life pours forth to meet him.
> The life that he himself has placed in it
> And that now answers him from within
> To chisel blows or quiet finger stroke.
> So we collaborate with God on his work of art.[2]

Distinctively from the human artist, the Divine Artist collaborates with His living image, which stirs underneath His forming hand. As the Lord's artwork, we can respond with acquiescence or resistance to His "chisel blows" and "quiet finger stroke." We think of the chisel blow of Stein's mother cutting off communication after Stein's entrance into Carmel. We see the finger strokes of God's gentle and incessant call to Stein to seek the Truth and find its Source. Through both types of crafting the Divine Artist is calling Stein to holiness and uniting her ever more fully to Him. The resulting artwork of each individual soul, so formed by the eternal Artist, reveals His incomparable beauty and handiwork.

Stein again describes human formation in artistic terms in what is thought to be her last known poem, presumably written in the summer of 1942, entitled "And I Remain with You." The speaker of this poem addresses a penetrating series of questions to God about His identity and His self-revelation. The poem concludes by celebrating His Divine artistry and our collaborative response:

> 5. Are you the master who builds the eternal cathedral,
> Which towers from the earth through the heavens?
> Animated by you, the columns are raised high

And stand immovably firm.
Marked with the eternal name of God,
They stretch up to the light,
Bearing the dome
That crowns the holy cathedral,
Your work that encircles the world:
Holy Spirit—God's molding hand!

6. Are you the one who created the unclouded mirror
Next to the Almighty throne,
Like a crystal sea,
In which Divinity lovingly looks at itself?
You bend over the fairest works of your creation,
And radiantly your own gaze
Is illumined in return.
And of all creatures the pure beauty
Is joined in one in the dear form
Of the Virgin, your immaculate bride:
Holy Spirit—Creator of all!

7. Are you the sweet song of love
And of holy awe
That eternally resounds around the triune throne,
That weds in itself the clear chimes of each and every being?
The harmony,
That joins together the members to the Head,
In which each one
Finds the mysterious meaning of being blessed
And joyously surges forth,
Freely dissolved in your surging:
Holy Spirit—eternal jubilation![3]

At the end of her sixth stanza, Stein celebrates the pure beauty of the Virgin Mary. In Our Lady we encounter the resplendent beauty manifested by a soul whose will is perfectly united to the plan of the Divine Artist. Our Lady corresponds completely with the Lord's will and purpose for her life. In the figure of the Blessed Virgin, God's idea for His artwork results in a pure and immaculate union between His plan and its manifestation in her life. Our Lady's soul is united perfectly to the Divine Being by grace, and her beauty thus surpasses that of all creatures: "the pure beauty / Is joined in one in the dear form / Of the Virgin."[4]

This splendor manifested by the human soul radiating union with God's plan and purpose ultimately exceeds that of the material image. Through such a person, Stein asserts in her culminating philosophical work *Finite and Eternal Being*, we encounter the "splendor which grace pours out over a human soul ... drawn near to the divine being in an entirely new sense."[5] The effect is radiance. The beauty of such an image "surpasses all purely natural brightness and harmony."[6] In her final spiritual work *The Science of the Cross*, Stein calls this human artwork a "living image," declaring that "living images (*lebendige Bilder*) are even better than those of wood or stone."[7]

The beauty of a life of holiness radiates for us with the sublime echoes of eternity in all its divine splendor. Fr. Guy Nicholls captures the splendor of the eternal manifested in both natural beauty and personal sanctity in *Unearthly Beauty: The Aesthetic of St. John Henry Newman*. Newman's "beauty of holiness" mirrors Stein's concept of the "living image":

> The clearest sign of beauty we can encounter in this life, which shows its connection to the divine and focuses our attraction on its hidden origin, is holiness. "A really holy man, a true saint," says Newman, "has a sort of secret power in him to attract others to him who are like-minded, and to influence all who have anything in them like him ... the *beauty* of holiness ... consists in tender and eager affection towards our Lord and Savior ... in the case of the Christian, what beauty of person is to the outward man."[8]

Stein and Newman are aesthetic soulmates in their regard for the ontological origin of beauty and its unearthly power. While Stein does not reference Newman directly to reinforce her argument, an emphasis on Newman's viewpoint is fitting, as Stein lovingly translated a significant amount of Newman's works from English into German during her intellectual and spiritual journey. Both saints are awed by the hidden, eternal origin of the beauty of holiness. Nicholls concludes:

> Since beauty originates in God and proceeds from him, all that participates in beauty draws it from God, while manifesting it in various ways. While the beauty of the natural world demonstrates the majesty of God, albeit in a shadowy way, the clearest sign of beauty we can encounter in this life, which shows its connection to the divine forces and focuses our attraction on its hidden origin, is holiness.[9]

Stein describes this beauty manifested through the soul's union with God, in her 1938 poem "I Will Remain with You," as a beauty before which "All we can do is be amazed and stammer and fall silent / Because intellect and words fail."[10]

Fittingly, Stein's encounter with a series of living images was foremost among the many influences which compelled Stein on her path to conversion. The real human beings with whom Stein came into contact disclosed to her the fullness of meaning, the divine presence, in both subtle and striking ways. Through them, and through her encounter with that most striking beauty of the human soul drawn near to the divine being by grace, Stein's own soul was transformed.

Stein first came into daily contact with a series of living images during her years of philosophical study in the Phenomenological Movement at Göttingen. In this milieux, she encountered the vibrant Christian witness of the many believers, as well as converts, who took part in this philosophical group. From her "beloved Master" Edmund Husserl, to her mentor Adolf Reinach and his wife Anna, her professor Max Scheler, as well as her future godmother Hedwig Conrad-Martius, Stein's intellectual society was full of men and women whose personal witness played a formative role in her own vocation. The effect of these living images was subtle, and occurred over time, but gradually the light of faith began to penetrate Edith's searching soul:

> This was my first encounter with this hitherto totally unknown world. It did not lead me as yet to the Faith. But it did

open for me a region of "phenomena" which I could then no longer bypass blindly. With good reason we were repeatedly enjoined to observe all things without prejudice, to discard all possible "blinders." The barriers of rationalistic prejudices with which I had unwittingly grown up fell, and the world of faith unfolded before me. Persons with whom I associated daily, whom I esteemed and admired, lived in it. At the least, they deserved my giving it some serious reflection. For the time being, I did not embark on a systematic investigation of the questions of faith; I was far too busy with other matters. I was content to accept without resistance the stimuli coming from my surroundings, and so, almost without noticing it, became gradually transformed.[11]

Three transformative encounters with living images provide distinct occasions of growth in Stein's vocational search for the Truth. These three encounters include the woman with the market basket, Anna Reinach's embrace of the Cross, and St. Teresa of Avila's uncompromising faith.

On the same visit to Frankfurt in which Stein was transfixed by the Flemish Passion sculpture in the museum exhibit, she was, in fact, even more deeply moved by a personal example of faith which she encountered in the Frankfurt Cathedral:

> The deepest impressions were made on me by things other than the Römerweg and the Hirschgraben. We stopped in at the cathedral for a few minutes; and, while we looked around in respectful silence, a woman carrying a market basket came in and knelt down in one of the pews to pray briefly. This was something entirely new to me. To the synagogues or to the Protestant churches which I had visited, one went only for services. But here was someone interrupting her everyday shopping errands to come into this church, although no other person was in it, as though she were here for an intimate conversation. I could never forget that.[12]

This woman, this living image, will never know the influence her simple act of devotion had on Stein's interior understanding of a personal relationship with Christ. Stein realized that the woman praying during her busy day of errands was speaking to another Person, although Stein did not yet have an intimate relationship with her Lord.

Stein experiences another life-changing encounter, this time with the Cross of Christ, at the end of World War I. Her beloved professor, Adolf Reinach, is killed in action, and Reinach's widow, Anna, asks Stein to assist her in putting Reinach's academic work in order. Stein hesitates in her response, uneasy about the suffering she will encounter. However, when Stein arrives, she meets a composed, believing, accepting widow. In Anna, Stein encounters a woman embracing the piercing Cross of Christ with resignation and courageous love:

> When, in 1918, she assisted Frau Anna Reinach in putting order to Adolf Reinach's literary legacy, Edith came face to face with the power of Christ's Cross at work in those who believed in Him. Edith expected her mentor's widow would be devastated by her loss. Instead, as the Reinach's had become Christians not long before Adolf's death, Anna displayed such courage and acceptance of her bereavement that Edith acknowledged the source of this strength.[13]

In this encounter with the suffering acceptance of Christ's Cross, Stein's unbelief is transformed. She proclaims:

> This was my first encounter with the Cross and the divine strength that it inspires in those who bear it. For the first time I saw before my very eyes the Church, born of Christ's redemptive suffering, victorious over the sting of death. It was the moment when my unbelief was shattered, Judaism paled, and Christ radiated before me: Christ in the mystery of the Cross ... Therefore at my clothing I could express no other desire than that of being called in the Order, "of the Cross."[14]

Stein's life, vocation, and ultimately her name, are radically transformed through this encounter with Anna Reinach, a living image. When Stein takes her religious name, she asks to include "of the Cross" in her title, in honor of this life-defining experience. Her religious name presents a constant remembrance of her encounter with the Cross, through which her unbelief was shattered by a living witness of faith.

One final living image must now speak to Stein's heart as her search for the Truth is fulfilled. Stein tells us that her search for the truth had become an interior state of being: "My longing for truth was a prayer in itself."[15] Truth will ultimately reveal Himself to Stein through His servant, the foundress of the Discalced Carmelite Order, St. Teresa of Avila.

Stein's decisive encounter with St. Teresa came in the summer of 1921, while on a visit to philosopher friends Hedwig Conrad-Martius and her husband in the vacation town of Bad Bergzabern. Stein is invited to spend an evening enjoying the family library while her hosts go out for the night. Happy to comply, she selects by providential chance the autobiography of St. Teresa of Avila, and she is transfixed. She is not mesmerized by a set of statutes, or by the force of argument, but by her living encounter with this towering saint. Stein reads the book cover to cover through the night, closing it at dawn, and declares that her encounter with St. Teresa of Avila "put an end to my long search for the true faith,"[16] recounting:

> I picked at random and took out a large volume. It bore the title *The Life of St. Teresa of Avila*, written by herself. I began to read, was at once captivated, and did not stop till I reached the end. As I closed the book, I said, "This is the truth."[17]

Stein's novice director and Mother Prioress of the Cologne Carmel, Sr. Teresia Renata Posselt, OCD, explains, "Day was breaking. Edith hardly noticed it. God's hand was upon her and she did not turn from Him."[18]

The very next day Stein buys a Catholic catechism and missal and studies them intensely. Then, for the first time in her life she enters a Catholic church to attend Mass, at the parish church of St. Martin. After hearing Mass, she requests baptism, and the parish priest finds her well prepared:

> Nothing was strange to me. Thanks to my previous study, I understood even the smallest ceremonies. The priest, a saintly-looking old man, went to the altar and offered the holy sacrifice reverently and devoutly. After Mass I waited until he made his thanksgiving. I followed him to the presbytery and asked him without more ado for baptism. He looked astonished and answered that one had to be prepared before being received into the Church. "How long have you been receiving instruction and who has been giving it?" The only reply I could make was, "Please, your reverence, test my knowledge."[19]

The reception of the Sacrament of Baptism in the Church of St. Martin, Bad Bergzabern, on 1 January 1922, marks Stein's formal conversion to Catholicism. On her baptismal day, she takes the names of St. Teresa, her soulmate in faith, and of her godmother, Hedwig Conrad-Martius:

> The parish records show she took the Christian names Teresa Hedwig, in acknowledgement of the special soul-bonding she had with St. Teresa of Avila, whose autobiography led the way to the ritual of entrance into the Catholic Church, as well as with her philosopher friend.[20]

Stein's resolve to enter the Carmelite Order dates from the moment of her encounter with St. Teresa. However, her spiritual director, Canon Josef Schwind, advises against immediate entry into religious life. He wisely advises that Stein needs to gain her bearings as a newly baptized Catholic, and he recommends a period of waiting while pursuing her apostolate in the world.

From the first moments of her conversion, Stein is abandoned to Divine Providence, and she acquiesces to this spiritual guidance, although "an attraction to live out her baptismal commitment as a member of the Discalced Carmelite Order, and so as a daughter of Teresa of Jesus, was inseparable from her resolve to enter the Church."[21] Stein will remain in the Catholic professional world as a teacher and lecturer for another 11 years before fulfilling her ultimate desire to enter Carmel. As her Mother Prioress tells us:

> Her innermost desire compelled her to the final surrender of a life devoted to God. But Canon Schwind, her spiritual advisor, would not hear of her entering an order for the time being. However, he gladly offered to find her a peaceful occupation that would allow her to live in conventual surroundings, where she could apply herself undisturbed to her studies and at the same time deepen her spiritual life. He introduced her to the Dominican convent school of St. Magdalena in Speyer.[22]

Throughout her years at St. Magdalena's, Stein is sought after frequently as a lecturer throughout Germany and in other countries. She fulfills a heavy schedule of teaching as well as traveling to conferences and giving radio addresses. These lectures form the content of Stein's teaching on the spiritual formation of the person and the vocation of woman, now collected into the work *Essays on Woman*. In her lecture entitled "Fundamental Principles of Women's Education," Stein emphasizes a central motif of her teaching, to be led by the Lord's guidance:

> What we can and must do is open ourselves to grace; that means to renounce our own will completely and give it captive to the divine will, to lay our whole soul, ready for reception and formation, into God's hands.[23]

This entrustment to the Lord is not a single action, but a daily, repeated handing over of our lives to Him. With great practical wisdom, honed through her years of experience seeking holiness while living as a Catholic professional in the world, Stein advises the soul:

> And when no outer rest whatever is attainable, when there is no place in which to retreat, if pressing duties prohibit a quiet hour, then at least she must for a moment seal off herself inwardly against all other things and take refuge in the Lord. He is indeed there and can give us in a single moment what we need.

Thus the remainder of the day will continue, perhaps in great fatigue and laboriousness, but in peace. And when night comes, and retrospect shows that everything was patchwork and much which one had planned left undone, when so many things rouse shame and regret, then take all as it is, lay it in God's hands, and offer it up to Him. In this way we will be able to rest in Him, actually to rest, and to begin the new day like a new life.[24]

Stein goes before us on the path to holiness; she understands the reality of the effort, the difficulties we face, and our need for grace. She presents throughout her lectures a clarion call to each soul to fully become the individual envisioned by Our Lord. The Catholic world benefits from these years of Stein's waiting for Carmel, through her invaluable contributions to Catholic intellectual thought.

Stein as Living Image

In his homily during the canonization ceremony of St. Teresa Benedicta of the Cross, Edith Stein, celebrated in St. Peter's Square on Sunday, 11 October 1998, the Holy Father offered the following testament to Stein's holiness:

> The cross of Christ! Ever blossoming, the tree of the cross continues to bear new fruits of salvation. This is why believers look with confidence to the cross, drawing from its mystery of love the courage and strength to walk faithfully in the footsteps of the crucified and risen Christ. Thus the message of the cross has entered the hearts of so many men and women and changed their lives.
>
> The spiritual experience of Edith Stein is an eloquent example of this extraordinary interior renewal. A young woman in search of the truth has become a saint and martyr through the silent workings of divine grace: Teresa Benedicta of the Cross, who from heaven repeats to us today all the words that marked her life: "Far be it from me to glory except in the cross of our Lord Jesus Christ."[25]

As Stein came to such interior renewal in response to her encounter with eternal Truth, she discovers that Truth is a Person. In response, she offers her life in wholehearted surrender to this Person, Jesus Christ:

> At the beginning she devoted herself to freedom. For a long time Edith Stein was a seeker. Her mind never tired of searching and her heart always yearned for hope. She traveled the arduous path of philosophy with passionate enthusiasm. Eventually she was rewarded: she seized the truth. Or better: she was seized by it. Then she discovered that truth had a name: Jesus Christ. From that moment on, the incarnate Word was her One and All. Looking back as a Carmelite on this period of her life, she wrote to a Benedictine nun: "Whoever seeks the truth is seeking God, whether consciously or unconsciously."[26]

Ironically, it is the Nazi persecution which allows Stein to enter the cloister of Carmel. When anti-Semitic laws make it impossible for Stein to hold a teaching position in Germany, her spiritual director, Abbot Raphael Walzer, OSB, agrees that the time is right for her to follow the footsteps of St. Teresa. Stein's entire spiritual journey from this moment forward becomes a deepening holocaust. She becomes for us a living witness through her fidelity to Christ in the face of ultimate persecution.

The looming clouds of the Nazi threat are darkening quickly around Stein and her family. The strain on Stein's relationship with her extended family is further deepened by their suspicions of her motives for conversion. What for Stein is a sincere pursuit of the Truth is seen by outsiders as a convenient attempt to escape the Jewish fate. This family distrust is painfully evident as Stein encounters her niece, Suzanne, at an appointment at the dentist shortly before Stein's final leaving home for Carmel:

> Susel was twelve years old at the time, but mature and thoughtful beyond her years. I had never been permitted to talk to the children about my conversion, but by now Erna had told them everything: for this I was grateful.

> I asked the child to visit Grandmother after I was gone. She promised to do so.
>
> "Why are you doing this now?" she asked.
>
> I understood very clearly what kind of parental discussions she had witnessed.[27]

Such moments were forming the future saint in deep interior abandonment. "I had to take that step in the complete darkness of faith," Stein says of her departure for Carmel.[28]

Stein's last day at home is October 12th, her birthday. The next morning, after attending early Mass, Stein bids farewell to her family, all of whom except for Rosa she is bidding farewell for the final time on this earth:

> When I embraced Erna, my mother wept aloud. I left quickly; Rosa and Else followed. When the trolley on which we were riding passed our house, there was no one at the window as on other occasions to wave a last farewell.
>
> At the station we had to wait a short time for the train to arrive. Else clung to me. After I had reserved a seat for myself, I went to the window and looked down at my sisters. I was struck by the difference in the two faces. Rosa was so serene as if she were going along into the tranquility of the convent. Else on the other hand, in her grief suddenly resembled an old woman.
>
> Finally the train began to move. Both waved as long as we could get even a glimpse of each other. So what I had scarcely yet hoped for would now become reality. I could not feel any wild joy. The scene I had just left behind was too terrible for that. But I felt a deep peace in the harbor of the divine will.[29]

Safely arrived in Cologne, Stein attends first vespers on 14 October 1933, in the chapel of the Carmel, in honor of the next day's Feast of St. Teresa of Avila. After vespers, she is accompanied by a friend of the Carmel and her god-child to the door of the enclosure, recounting: "At last it opened, and in deep peace I crossed the threshold into the House of the Lord."[30]

Her daily witness of heroic faith, hope, and charity, lived out in moments such as these within her family, and within her cloistered community, were presented to the Church for official recognition. Stein's Cause for Canonization, in fact, was initially opened as a straightforward cause for sanctity. The Church subsequently re-opened Stein's Cause as a martyrdom Cause when evidence of her ultimate and total witness for the faith became apparent. Her death completes the testimony of her life of faith, in which "the last chapter has to be lived, to be written, spoken with her blood."[31]

The power of martyrdom, communicated through the very meaning of the word as an act of witness or testimony,[32] is emphasized in the *Catechism of the Catholic Church*:

> *Martyrdom* is the supreme witness given to the truth of the faith: it means bearing witness even unto death. The martyr bears witness to Christ who died and rose, to whom he is united by charity. He bears witness to the truth of the faith and of Christian doctrine.[33]

Stein prophetically understood the power of her immolation, despite its apparent futility in the face of Nazi power. She believed that her life and sufferings could be offered both for the conversion of her Jewish people and as a counter-influence to the rampant evils of her time. As she wrote in a letter to a Benedictine religious in 1930, "After every encounter in which I am made aware how powerless we are to exercise direct influence, I have a deeper sense of the urgency of my own *holocaustum*."[34] Stein formally expressed her desire to offer herself for Christ in a request to her Mother Superior at the Echt Carmel, on Passion Sunday, in March 1939:

> Dear Mother: please will Your Reverence allow me to offer myself to the heart of Jesus as a sacrifice of propitiation for true peace, that the domain of the Antichrist may collapse, if possible, without a new world war, and that a new order may be established? I would like it (my request) granted this very day because it is the twelfth hour. I know that I am a nothing, but Jesus desires it, and surely he will call many others to do likewise in these days.[35]

The Living Image

In her self-offering to the Lord, Stein identifies with the figure of Queen Esther of the Old Testament who stands as an intercessor for the Jewish people before the King. She writes to a fellow religious in 1938:

> I also trust in the Lord's having accepted my life for all of them. I keep having to think of Queen Esther who was taken from among her people precisely that she might represent them before the king. I am a very poor and powerless little Esther, but the King who chose me is infinitely great and merciful. That is such a great comfort.[36]

When she is arrested at the Echt Carmel on 2 August 1942, Stein steps into the street and encourages her sister, "Come Rosa, we go for our people."[37] This statement, evoking her connection with the Old Testament Queen, reveals Stein's awareness of the efficacious role of her sufferings and ensuing death. As a living image, she asks each of us:

> Do you want to be totally united to the Crucified? If you are serious about this, you will be present, by the power of His Cross, at every front, at every place of sorrow, bringing to those who suffer comfort, healing, and salvation.[38]

Her readiness for martyrdom and her internal union with Christ in laying down her life for Him are critical elements in Stein's recognition as a martyr of the Catholic faith. When she is arrested in 1942, she had already written a moving letter to His Holiness Pope Pius XI, urging him to advocate on behalf of the Jewish people in their persecution under National Socialism. The letter, written in 1933 before Stein's entrance into Carmel, manifests her prophetic understanding that silence before the persecution of the Jews would enable future persecution of the Christian faith:

> For the time being, the fight against Catholicism will be conducted quietly and less brutally than against Jewry, but no less systematically. It won't take long before no Catholic will be able

to hold office in Germany unless he dedicates himself unconditionally to the new course of action.[39]

Although Stein had entered the Carmel in Cologne, Germany, she is not able to live her remaining days there undisturbed. In fact, she had a premonition that persecution would find her even behind the cloister walls. In April of 1935, on the day of her profession of vows, Sr. Teresia Benedicta of the Cross visited with guests for the occasion. One visitor remarked:

> During our conversation I happened to remark that probably she would be safe here in Carmel. To this she very quickly replied: *"Oh no, I don't believe that. Surely they will come and take me out of here. In any case I cannot count on being left here in peace."*[40]

The events of Kristallnacht, three years later, on 9 November 1938, would confirm Stein's fears. On that "Night of Broken Glass," synagogues throughout Germany were burnt, Jewish businesses destroyed, and Jews and their families were attacked. It was no longer safe for Stein to remain in Germany. Plans are made for her transfer to a Carmel in Echt, the Netherlands.

In a letter from Cologne dated 9 December 1938, Stein details the upheaval of her family members, who have begun emigrating to the United States, South America, and Norway. Four of the seven Stein siblings (Elfriede, Paul, Rosa, and Edith) do not escape the Nazi terror and will die in concentration camps. Stein also suffers the necessary separation from her religious family, as she must leave her Carmel as well as her country for her own safety and that of her Order:

> I must tell you that I already brought my religious name with me into the house as a postulant, I receive it exactly as I requested it. By the cross I understood the destiny of God's people which, even at that time, began to announce itself. I thought that those who recognized it as the cross of Christ had to take it upon themselves in the name of all. Certainly, today I know more of what it means to be wedded to the Lord in the sign of the Cross.

> ... I do not know yet what will happen about the publication. Should it become possible, after all, it would be my farewell gift to Germany.
>
> ... As the atmosphere around us grows steadily darker, all the more must we open our hearts for the light from above.[41]

Stein is taken across the border by car under cover of darkness on the night of 31 December 1938. During her escape she makes a request, despite the danger of delay, to visit the ancient shrine of Mary, Queen of Peace, as she departs from Cologne. Her visit to this sacred church and to the holy statue of Our Lady under the same title is fortuitous. A few short years after Stein's departure, the Cologne Carmel suffers complete destruction by bombing. The Order is eventually re-established under the auspices of the Queen of Peace at the ancient, holy site at which Stein had interceded for her Order, beseeching Our Lady to watch over her religious family, as she herself fled from deadly danger.

Stein's bold resistance in the face of the encroaching threat of National Socialism continued throughout her remaining years in the Echt cloister. It soon becomes clear that Stein and her sister Rosa, who has also converted to Catholicism and joined the community as an extern sister, will be safer in Switzerland. An attempt is made to transfer the two sisters to a Carmel in Le Pâquier. When they apply for an exit visa for the transfer, Stein is summoned to the Gestapo office in Maastrich for questioning. As she enters the police headquarters, Stein greets the officers with the bold proclamation, "Praised be Jesus Christ!"[42] With this fearless testimony, Stein offers a direct witness to her faith despite the danger to her safety. As her first biographer, Sr. Teresia Renata Posselt, OCD, recounts:

> Startled by this greeting (the officers) looked up but they did not reply. (Later she explained to Reverend Mother that she had felt driven to behave as she had done, knowing well enough that it was imprudent from a human standpoint, because she saw quite clearly that this was no mere question

of politics but was part of the eternal struggle between Jesus and Lucifer.[43]

On Sunday, 26 July 1942, a pastoral letter condemning the deportation of the Jews is read from every Catholic pulpit in the Netherlands in a coordinated act of resistance of the Dutch Catholic Church. The letter is a clear and direct protest of the anti-Semitic measures in force. It reads, in part:

> The undersigned church communities of the Netherlands, deeply shaken by the measures taken against the Jews in the Netherlands that have excluded them from participation in the normal life of the people, have learned with horror of the latest regulations by which men, women, children and whole families are to be deported to the territory of the German Reich.[44]

Nazi retribution against this act of defiance by the Dutch Catholic Church is swift and lethal. A round up which targets converts from Judaism to Catholicism is enacted on August 2nd. Stein and her sister Rosa are victims of the round-up:

> All non-Aryan members of every Dutch religious community were arrested and taken away. In Echt there was no hint of what was about to happen. At five in the afternoon the Sisters had assembled in choir for meditation; Sr. Benedicta was just reading out the point for meditation when two rings at the turn were heard ... There were two officers asking for Sister Stein.[45]

Stein and her sister, Rosa, are given five minutes to prepare to leave the convent and then are taken away by the police. In these harrowing last moments with her religious community, Stein begs for prayers:

> Sr. Benedicta returned to the Choir. She knelt reverently in front of the Blessed Sacrament and then left the Choir with the whispered words, "Please pray, Sisters!"[46]

A crowd has gathered, and a police van is waiting at the corner, when Stein and her sister, Rosa, step out into the street. We learn of the self-sacrificial words with which Stein embraces her unknown fate through archivist Sr. M. Amata Neyer, OCD:

> A friend of the Carmel who had been quickly called to the scene was able to get so close to the two arrested women that they could clearly hear Edith's exhortation to her weeping sister Rosa: "Come, let us go for our people!"[47]

From the moment of her arrest, Stein begins her Way of the Cross with Christ. Arrested on a Sunday, Stein is transported through a series of holding camps to Auschwitz Concentration Camp. She manages to send small bits of news and a few short notes back to her sisters in Echt. From these, we glean a glimpse of her interior state. She writes on 4 August, two days after her arrest:

> During the past night we left the transit station A. (Amersfoot) and landed here early this morning ... All the Catholics are here together ... We are very calm and cheerful. Of course, so far there has been no Mass and Communion; maybe that will come later. Now we have a chance to experience a little how to live purely from within.[48]

A final note from the barracks at Westerbork Camp, on 6 August, details Stein's spiritual focus:

> Early tomorrow a transport leaves ... What is most necessary: woolen stockings, two blankets. For Rosa all the warm underwear and whatever was in the laundry; for us both towels and wash cloths. Rosa also has no toothbrush, no Cross and no rosary. I would like the next volume of the breviary (so far I have been able to pray gloriously). Our identity cards, registration cards [as Jews], and ration cards.[49]

The transport to Auschwitz departed on Friday, 7 August. Stein's final journey takes her back across Germany, through some of the towns in which she has lived, to her ultimate destination.

"We are Heading East"

The train car holding Stein is known to have stopped at the Station of Schifferstadt, near to Speyer. Stein is able to send a message from the platform. As recorded in Sr. M. Amata Neyer's *Edith Stein: Her Life in Photos and Documents*, "A number of witnesses have stated that a woman dressed in dark clothing, who called herself Edith Stein, gave them a short message orally or even in writing: 'We are on the road to the east!'"[50] The station master, Valentin Fouqué, and other eye witnesses, have testified that Stein sent greetings to the Schwind family of Speyer, and also to the religious sisters of nearby St. Magdalena's Dominican Convent, where she had lived and taught before entering Carmel. Stein's repeated message, "We are heading East," is prophetic. Perhaps the most poignant of these final testimonies arrives to Sr. Placida Laubhardt, OSB, who was also "non-Aryan" and later interned in Ravensbrück Concentration Camp. She testifies that "she had received the note; that it was unmistakably in Edith's handwriting; and that she had burned it a few days before her own arrest, to protect her community. The actual wording, according to Sr. Placida, was 'Grüße von Sr. Teresia Benedicta a Cruce. Unterwegs *ad orientem*' or 'Greetings from Sr. Teresia Benedicta a Cruce. En route to the East.'"[51]

With her final recorded words, Stein speaks both a literal statement of the destination of the transport, as well as a testament to her ultimate hope in Our Lord's Resurrection. Offering her life *in testimonium fidei*, she unites herself to Christ's sacrifice, entrusting the *holocaustum* of her life to God. She points us "*ad orientem*," "to the East" in our own journey of holiness, offering ourselves to Him with sacrificial hope in all things.

Her earthly journey concludes at Auschwitz on Sunday, 9 August 1942, the day now celebrated as her Feast Day on the Church calendar. With the members of the transport, Stein is killed by gassing with Zyklin-B in a small white farmhouse on the edge of the camp. A white stone from that farmhouse is enshrined in the crypt of the Carmelite convent church Mary Queen of Peace, in Cologne. Biographer Freda Mary Oben details the last days and hours of Stein's life:

> During the night of August 6–7th, the transport left Hooghalen Station (from Westerbork Camp). It was the First Friday and the remembrance of the Feast of the Sacred Heart.
>
> It is recorded that the train carried 987 souls, among which were 120 baptized Jews ... When the train arrived on August 9th, 559 persons dismounted. If the original figure of 987 passengers is correct, it can only mean that either 426 persons were discharged elsewhere, which is highly unlikely since the trains went directly to Auschwitz, or that they perished during the two terrible days on the train.
>
> They were divided into two groups: 264 persons in one group, Edith and Rosa among them, were gassed and burned in a pit that very day. They never entered the camp. They had walked about 15 minutes through a grove where they were told to disrobe and leave their things. They were brought to a white cottage, formerly a farmer's home, where the doors and windows were boarded up for the gassing with Zyklin B. I have always thought that when Edith entered the cottage, she was carrying a small child.
>
> Her labors are over. She climbed the mountain to the top. With Christ, she was nailed to the Cross.[52]

Her death in witness to the Catholic Faith, furthermore, is clearly detailed in the extensive documentation prepared for the process of Stein's canonization cause. The *Positio Super Martyrio et Super Virtutibus Canonizationis Servae Dei Teresiae Benedictae a Cruce*, documenting Stein's canonization, presents the evidence of Stein's martyrdom. Although Stein's Cause for Sanctity was initially opened as the Cause of an individual who had lived a life of heroic faith, hope, and charity, further evidence surfaced during the Cause's initial proceedings which proved that Stein was killed *in odium fidei*, in hatred of the faith. Her Cause was then re-opened as a Cause for Martyrdom. The relator of Stein's Cause, Fr. Ambrose Eszer, OP, states:

> The splendid evidence of the heroic virtues of the Servant of God, highlights not only her love of God but also her readiness for total sacrifice, beyond the admirable perseverance necessary for Christian martyrdom"[53]

Why should Stein be specially recognized for a death suffered by so many millions of Jews? What makes her death a cause of sanctity? The answer lies in the motive for Stein's martyrdom. Fr. Eszer notes in the *Positio* that while the "informal" cause of Stein's martyrdom "presents itself as the fundamental unity of the hatred of the National Socialists against Catholicism and Judaism," the "formal and immediate cause of the deportation and consequent killing of Catholic Jews of Holland was the wish to punish the Catholic Church for its protest, therefore *odium fidei* and not hatred of the race."[54] This distinction between the informal and formal cause of Stein's death is pivotal. Stein dies *in odium fidei*, directly due to hatred of the Nazi regime for the Catholic faith, the necessary qualification for a Catholic martyr.

We must properly recognize Stein as a martyr, furthermore, to give voice to the many silent martyrs of the modern age. The insidious characteristic of modern martyrdom is that the "Tyrant" denies the victim the opportunity to proclaim the faith for which they are being killed. While Stein lacked any formal opportunity to make a profession of faith in the face of her martyrdom, the *Positio* affirms that "the *Provocatio* of the 'Tyrant,' was constituted by the action of the Dutch Bishops to which the Servant of God undoubtedly adhered given that she had always criticized, even radically, a weak response to National Socialism."[55] Furthermore, it is clear that Stein was interiorly ready to offer her life. As the *Positio* declares, "Regarding her spiritual preparation for martyrdom, furthermore, there can be no doubt because she consciously offered herself as a victim for the conversion of the Jews and for peace."[56]

In ancient times the persecuted Christian was brought into the arena and asked to publicly profess their faith in Christ. At that moment, before the Tyrant, the Christian proclaimed fidelity in public witness. Today, the modern Tyrant fears allowing such public witness to the Christian martyr. Christians disappear, they are killed without a trial, they are removed from their jobs, they are silenced *in odium fidei*, but the motive is not declared openly. The modern Tyrant and his henchmen operate in shadow, remaining faceless, and the goal is to deprive the Christian of the power of any testimony. In his prescient testament to the new martyrs of the modern age, Catholic author Robert Royal emphasizes this insidious twist in the fate of the witnesses of our time:

> Most of the hundreds of thousands of people killed for their faith in the modern world are not known by name. Even where the local churches have tried to keep track of who disappeared, many people simply vanished into the maw of various killing machines. In Latin America, for example, "to disappear" became a verb used in a new way, e.g., "three religious were *disappeared*." People were classified as *desaparecidos* ("disappeareds"). The neologisms tell us that something new about the modern world was perceived by those who experienced its injustices. Systematic and secret elimination of groups of people became common toward the end of the second Christian millennium.[57]

In the documentation for Stein's canonization cause, the Holy Innocents are presented as the precursors to these modern silent witnesses to the faith, killed for Christ without a voice:

> National Socialism, in all of its persecutions of the Church, not only did not want to provoke but wanted to suppress every possible confession of faith which their actions would have "provoked," and to reduce the persecuted to the state of children who cannot express their faith, an extreme humiliation of their dignity ... According to the teaching of the Church, the Holy Innocents of Bethlehem are also true martyrs.[58]

Stein's martyrdom is emblematic of the many victims of modern persecution whose testimony is made in silence, yet is fully witness at the same time:

> Although the Church must not too easily confer the title of martyr, she must neither on the other hand give advantage to the modern "Tyrants" who, with their sophisticated machinations and their evil tricks, seek to eliminate not only the Catholic faith but also martyrdom, rendering the Church and her witnesses completely *mute*."[59]

Through her declaration that she is "heading East" as she goes to her death for Christ, Stein points the way for us to follow. Her martyrdom in the death camps of Auschwitz is the fulfillment of the interior journey which she had consciously begun upon closing St. Teresa of Avila's autobiography and declaring, "This is the truth."[60] Her death as a martyr for the faith, for the Truth of Christ and His Cross, seals Stein's assertion and proclaims it eternally.

Notes

1. Edith Stein, "The Significance of Woman's Intrinsic Value in National Life," *Essays on Woman*, trans. Freda Mary Oben, Ph.D., ed. Dr. L. Gelber and Romaeus Leuven, OCD, 2nd rev. ed., *The Collected Works of Edith Stein*, Vol. 2 (Washington, DC: ICS Publications, 1996) 256.
2. Stein, from "I Am Always in Your Midst," in *The Hidden Life*, 119.
3. Stein, from "And I Remain with You," in *The Hidden Life*, 143–5.
4. Stein, from "And I Remain with You," in *The Hidden Life*, 143.
5. Edith Stein, *Finite and Eternal Being*, trans. Kurt F. Reinhardt, ed. Dr. L. Gelber and Romaeus Leuven, OCD, *The Collected Works of Edith Stein*, Vol 9 (Washington, DC: ICS Publications, 2002) 323.
6. Stein, *Finite*, 323.
7. Edith Stein, *The Science of the Cross: A Study of St. John of the Cross*, trans. Hilda Graef, ed. Dr. L. Gelber and Romaeus Leuven, OCD, (London: Burns and Oates, 1960) 209, (pg. 276 in ICS Publications edition).
8. Guy Nicholls, *Unearthly Beauty: The Aesthetic of St. John Henry Newman* (Herefordshire: Gracewing, 2019) 330.
9. Nicholls, *Unearthly Beauty*, 330.
10. Stein, "I Will Remain with You," *The Hidden Life*, 139.
11. Stein, *Life*, 260–1.
12. Stein, *Life*, 401.
13. Josephine Koeppel, OCD, "Chronology," in Stein, *Life*, 419–20.
14. Stien quoted in Teresia Renata Posselt, OCD, *Edith Stein: The Life of a Philosopher and Carmelite*, ed. Susanne M. Batzdorff, Josephine Koeppel, and John Sullivan (Washington, DC: ICS Publications, 2005) 59–60.
15. Stein as quoted in Posselt, *Edith Stein*, 63.
16. Edith Stein, "How I Came to the Cologne Carmel," in *Selected Writings: With Comments and Reminiscences*, trans. and ed. Susanne Batzdorff (Springfield, Illinois: Templegate Publishers, 1990) 19.
17. Stein as quoted in Posselt, 63.
18. Posselt, *Edith Stein*, 63.
19. Stein as quoted in Posselt, 64.
20. Posselt, 294.
21. Koeppel, Josephine, in "Chronology" to Stein's *Life*, 420.
22. Posselt, 65.
23. Stein, *Woman*, 143.

24. Stein, *Woman*, 143.
25. Pope John Paul II, "Homily at Canonization Eucharist," in *Holiness Befits Your House: Documentation on the Canonization of Edith Stein*, ed. John Sullivan, OCD (ICS Publications: Washington, DC: 2000) n. 1.
26. Pope John Paul II, "Homily at Canonization Eucharist," in *Holiness Befits Your House: Documentation on the Canonization of Edith Stein*, n. 5.
27. Stein as quoted in Posselt, 127.
28. Stein as quoted in Posselt, 126.
29. Stein as quoted in Posselt, 129.
30. Stein as quoted in Posselt, 130.
31. Steven Payne, OCD, "Edith Stein e S. Giovanni della Croce," Fall Lecture Series (Rome: Pontifical Gregorian University, 1999) 267, translation mine.
32. John A. Hardon (ed.), *Modern Catholic Dictionary*, "Etym. Greek *martyros*, witness, martyr," (Bardstown, KY: Eternal Life, 2001) 335.
33. *Catechism of the Catholic Church*, (Boston: Pauline Books and Media, 1994) n. 2473.
34. Stein, *Self-Portrait in Letters*, Letter 52, to Sr. Adelgundis Jaegerschmid, OSB.
35. Stein, *Self-Portrait in Letters*, Letter 296, to Mother Ottilia Thannisch, OCD.
36. Stein, *Self-Portrait in Letters*, Letter 281, to Mother Petra Brüning, OSU.
37. As quoted in Oben, *Life and Thought*, 60.
38. Edith Stein, from unpublished writing in the Cologne Archive, cited in Chronology to *Life in a Jewish Family*, 435.
39. Stein, "Letter to Pope Pius XI," 20 April 1933, as quoted in Posselt, *Edith Stein*, 313.
40. Posselt, *Edith Stein*, 163, italics given.
41. Stein, *Self-Portrait in Letters*, Letter 287, to Mother Petra Brüning, OSU.
42. Posselt, *Edith Stein*, 197.
43. Posselt, *Edith Stein*, 197–8.
44. "Letter of the Dutch Catholic Bishops," 20 July 1942, in Posselt, *Edith Stein*, 203.
45. Posselt, *Edith Stein*, 206–7.
46. Posselt, *Edith Stein*, 207.
47. Neyer, *Edith Stein: Her Life in Photos and Documents*, 74.
48. Stein, *Self-Portrait in Letters*, Letter 340, to Mother Ambrosia Antonia Engelmann, OCD.
49. Stein, *Self-Portrait in Letters*, Letter 342, to Mother Ambrosia Antonia Engelmann, OCD.

50. Neyer, 78.
51. Posselt, 340.
52. Freda Mary Oben, Ph.D., *The Life and Thought of Edith Stein* (New York: Alba House, 2001) 62–3.
53. *Positio Super Martyrio et Super Virtutibus*, "Praenotatio," 3, translation mine.
54. *Positio Super Martyrio et Super Virtutibus*, "Praenotatio," 3, 6, translation mine.
55. *Positio Super Martyrio et Super Virtutibus*, "Relatio," 57, translation mine.
56. *Positio Super Martyrio et Super Virtutibus*, "Relatio," 57, translation mine.
57. Robert Royal, *The Catholic Martyrs of the Twentieth Century: A Comprehensive World History*, (New York: The Crossroad Publishing Company, 2000) 10, italics given.
58. *Positio Super Martyrio et Super Virtutibus*, "Relatio," 57, translation mine.
59. *Positio Super Martyrio et Super Virtutibus*, "Relatio," 59, translation mine.
60. Stein as quoted in Posselt, *Edith Stein*, 63.

3 THE SOUL'S AWAKENING

> *Beauty ... insists that I inwardly open myself to it and let my inner self be determined by it. And for as long as this inner contact is not effected, for as long as I withhold the response which beauty requires, beauty doesn't entirely divulge itself to me.*
>
> Stein, *Philosophy of Psychology and the Humanities*[1]

Can a world that has lived through the horrors of the Holocaust still respond to beauty? Can a dulled and deadened soul be reawakened? Can we come alive anew? Can we encounter beauty, even unexpectedly, and be transformed? Yes. The soul of man can be renewed. Beauty has the power to restore our spirit. Beauty is insistent. We feel its demand within our soul to open ourselves to it and allow it to transform us. All the possibilities of the soul's awakening are offered through a proper encounter with beauty. The artwork can assist in bringing about this interior awakening.

From Hollow Men to Soul-Filled Living

In her illuminating philosophical investigation, *Finite and Eternal Being*, written in Carmel at the request of her religious superiors and published posthumously after the Second World War, Stein explains that the experience of beauty is a uniquely human experience. The human soul is distinguished by the ability to experience joy in beauty, and man's spiritual capacity is satisfied by beauty. We experience joy in beauty when its splendor touches our soul. But what if our soul has become untouchable? What if our soul exists in a deadened, indifferent state of being? Is this possible? Not only is an interior condition of indifference to beauty possible, Stein warns, but such indifference is an ever more frequent state of modern man's soul.

Stein begins to examine these ideas in 1919, after she has been working for nearly two years as assistant to Edmund Husserl. She submits two treatises on human creative achievement under the joint title of "Contributions Toward a Philosophical Grounding of Psychology and the Humanities," to the *Jahrbuch für Philosophie und phänomenologische Forschung* for a *Commemorative Edition* in honor of Husserl's sixtieth birthday. Publication of the volume, in fact, did not take place until 1922 due to economic setbacks.

Technical in content due to their composition as Stein's *Habilitationsschrift*, or second dissertation, required in applying for a university professorship, these treatises have been published in English as *Philosophy of Psychology and the Humanities*. Stein's treatises, referred to as both "the pinnacle of Stein's phenomenological thought," as well as her "most-significant pre-conversion writings,"[2] provide the "conceptual groundwork that is essential to understanding what the mature Stein would attempt in the two great works of her cloistered life," *Finite and Eternal Being* and *The Science of the Cross*.[3]

These texts present Stein's understanding of the human person, and in them she explains the role of the humanities in the formation of the human person, as well as the response which beauty requires of the human soul. She particularly emphasizes the insistence of beauty, and our soul's proper response to it:

> Beauty is not like the sensible qualities of the object to which beauty adheres. Those qualities place no claim upon me. I can perceive them, but I need not trouble myself further about them. Basically they don't matter to me. Beauty, on the other hand, insists that I inwardly open myself to it and let my inner self be determined by it.[4]

The beauty manifested in a pastoral landscape, for instance, evokes joy within me. I see the meadows and the rolling hills, and I am filled with aesthetic joy. The splendor of the landscape's beauty touches my soul. This response occurs within me, Stein explains, because "the value *requires* the attitude. My gladness is the 'response' to the beauty of the landscape that is tendering itself to me."[5] To observe that the beauty "requires" my response, means that "the attitude is rationally demanded by the value. This is not the same as saying that the value 'causes' the attitude with some sort of physical necessity."[6] In other words, beauty objectively requires a response from our soul. A non-response to beauty is not the result of a deficiency in the beauty but rather a deficiency in our ability to perceive the beauty or the openness of our soul towards the beauty, or both.

And yet, how often does beauty receive a lackluster response from us? We ignore it; we overlook it; we may even be threatened by it; and we reject it. Its insistence is lost on us. While beauty rationally demands a response, this proper response of our soul to beauty is by no means assured. Our response to beauty is neither automatic nor guaranteed. Our soul must be receptive to beauty so that we respond properly to it.

It is possible, in fact, to miss the impact of the beauty completely. It is entirely possible, Stein explains, for an individual to encounter beauty "without having any hunch that it's the bearer of a value" or even to be told "that it possesses a value, without catching sight of this value yourself."[7] When such a lackluster encounter with beauty occurs, "you as subject are value-blind."[8]

So, what causes this value-blindness? Are we, as a modern society, losing our spiritual vision? What happens if I miss the beauty before me due to a dulled spiritual vision? For Stein, it is possible to encounter beauty and have no interior reaction. "The beauty of the landscape can stand clearly before my eyes but leave me 'cold.'"[9] Have we felt this way at times? Unable to respond to the beauty before us? The beauty must necessarily be present for the experience of it to touch my soul. But Stein adds the further caveat: my soul must also exhibit openness and receptivity in order to be touched. "An inner condition of the subject must be added in order to render possible the acquisition of the value,"[10] she asserts.

The receptive human soul is a vital factor in the full experience of the beautiful. We must allow beauty to touch us interiorly. "And for as long as this inner contact is not effected," Stein explains, "for as long as I withhold the response which beauty requires, beauty doesn't entirely 'divulge itself to me.'"[11] An unfulfilled encounter with beauty? Yes. This is certainly possible. What could cause my soul to fail to respond to beauty as beauty demands? An inner deformation of man's spiritual capacity is possible, Stein warns. The quality of our soul differs from person to person, and our spiritual capacity also differs individually. "How you pick up values and how you behave toward them, how you enjoy things, how you make yourself happy, how you grieve and how you suffer: that all depends on the quality of your soul."[12]

To describe "this mysterious something, the soul," Stein maintains that "the human being lives out of his soul, which is the center of his being."[13] She goes on to explain that "your soul's being is like the core in which is rooted an individual as such, something indissoluble and unnamable."[14] It is from this inner spiritual core that we respond to a value such as beauty. Stein also distinguishes the mind from the soul, explaining, "With the mind we simply take on the world, but your soul takes up the world into itself. The world 'strikes a chord' within your soul, and in a special way in each individual soul."[15]

It is possible, however, for this interior core to be "switched off" inside a person, so that the individual no longer lives from the center of his being, but instead allows his soul's life to be "shoved into the background in favor of the peripheral."[16] We can remain on the surface in life, pushing aside anything which would penetrate to the depths of our being. We escape from the demands of beauty if we limit its access to our inner core. We can push beauty away through indifference, hostility, or even ignorance. We remain on the surface, and our deeper interior life runs dry.

With such an escape from the depths to a surface existence, moreover, comes consequences. Significantly, Stein warns, the personal quality of our human existence can be diminished. We can lose our individuality. "Where your soul is disconnected from the actuality of living," Stein tells us, "what's missing from behavior and from the visible being of the individual is the individual flair or, as we also say, the 'personal touch.'"[17] This piercing assessment of man's ability to lose his individuality might have been called by Stein, if she had lived in our age of social media, the Instagram Effect. This effect is seen in people who live not out of their own soul, with their own distinctive individuality, but who remain on the periphery, imbibing the images, emotions, and experiences of others in a superficial manner. "The individual's life becomes driven by sensory powers and perhaps by volition, or even carried along by the powers of someone else's soul,"[18] Stein asserts. We have all seen this effect, and its deadening impact upon the soul that loses its personal stamp, its individual spark. We have perhaps ourselves fallen prey to the hollowing effect of being carried along by others, in a swift and superficial current of experience.

When we switch off our individual spiritual capacity, when we remain on the periphery, we avoid our own interior life, and we avoid the depth from which we are meant to live. In such a situation, "the individual's living isn't coming out of the center of his or her own being, and therefore it is lacking the originality and authenticity of 'core-valent' living."[19] The saintly teenager, Blessed Carlo Acutis, famously commented on our modern tendency to exist in such borrowed reality. "All people are born as originals," he affirmed, "but many live as photocopies."[20] We become an artificial representation of ourselves, without the authentic core from which our life should be experienced. We become a human being, Stein states, whose "distinctiveness bears the stamp of artificiality."[21]

Such a state of superficial living is empty and lifeless. We recognize the symptoms in society of such soul-less living. We see the unhappiness, anger, and lack of empathy which result from the detachment of our inner spiritual core:

> The switching off of your soul is an arbitrary one. Its counterpart is a pervasive rigidity of your soul against all endeavors, a running dry of its life. The ego descends into its depths, it holes up there. Yet the ego meets up with a gaping void in there. The ego gets the feeling that it's missing its soul, that it's only a shadow of itself detached from its ownmost being … Kindliness no longer radiates in positive sentiments and kindly actions, and the interior seems emptied of everything that used to fill it, everything in which the individuality, itself ineffable, used to articulate itself.[22]

T. S. Eliot describes such souls that are only a shadow of themselves in "The Waste Land," as the speaker observes the lifeless crowd flowing over London Bridge. "So many," the speaker marvels, "I had not thought death had undone so many."[23] Eliot further examines the soulless condition of modern man in his poetic presentation of "The Hollow Men." These empty souls accost the audience and bemoan their dulled identity: "We are the hollow men / We are the stuffed men / Leaning together / Headpiece filled with straw. Alas!"[24] A loss of individuality marks these men with a pronounced despair and emptiness: "Our dried voices, when / We whisper together / Are quiet and meaningless / As wind in dry grass / Or rats' feet over broken glass / In our dry cellar."[25]

Both Stein and Eliot identify the running dry of life as the mark of the hollow existence. But this state of being is not a permanent condition. No! The soul is a fountain of life within the person. The core of the person can be "switched off," become shriveled and dry, but the soul of an individual can be renewed, switched back on, made again the center from which we experience and respond to reality:

> We can think to ourselves of individuals who are altogether missing their own center of their being, and together with it a genuine personality and (qualitative) individuality. With the *human being*, in all instances of "soul-less" behavior you'll be permitted only to say that he didn't find or temporarily lost "himself," for as long as his individuality is unrecognizable ... In principle he has such a center, which can burst forth at any time.[26]

Our individuality is ineffable. Our soul is eternal. It cannot be permanently extinguished, but only temporarily dimmed to a flicker. This interior dimming can be due to any number of reasons: indifference, fear, superficiality, emotional disturbance, trauma, exhaustion. We can wish we felt more deeply but find ourselves at the end of our strength. When the natural, life-giving power of the soul is exhausted, the soul no longer functions efficaciously:

> If the individual isn't living out of the depths, out of his soul, then these powers for his life get lost. And now it can also happen that your soul, without getting switched off, stops generating life. The source hidden in your soul can sputter out. The world still comes crashing in upon it, but your soul cannot "light up" inside. It has no "response" anymore. The susceptibility for values breaks down, although they can still be recognized.[27]

Stein personally understood this state of interior exhaustion which can overwhelm the soul so that it no longer lights up inside. During her search for the truth, for the ultimate meaning of life and existence, she began to despair of finding a satisfactory answer to her struggle. She could not solve her crisis through sheer force of will or intellect. Her inner battle gradually left Stein in a state of utter exhaustion and even indifference to continue living. She tottered on the brink of despair:

> This excruciating struggle to attain clarity was waged unceasingly inside me, depriving me of rest day and night ... Little by little I worked myself into a state of veritable despair. For the first time in my life I was confronted by

something I could not conquer by sheer will-power ... I had often boasted that my skull was harder than the thickest of walls, and now I was beating my forehead raw, yet the impregnable wall would not give in the least. All this brought me to a point where life itself seemed unbearable. ... I could no longer cross the street without wishing I would be run over by some vehicle. And when we went on an excursion, I hoped I would fall off a cliff and not return alive. Probably no one suspected how things stood with me.[28]

As we know, an encounter with the Cross of Christ shattered Stein's doubts and unbelief. Shortly after World War I, when she visited Anna Reinach, the widow of her beloved professor Adolf Reinach, Stein encountered the living, pulsating, loving, sacrificing heart of Christ on His Cross. This encounter was enabled through Anna's embrace of the piercing suffering of personal loss and widowhood, in union with Christ. In that encounter with Anna, who embraced the Cross and its life-giving power, the center of Stein's soul burst forth fully for the first time. "It was the moment when my unbelief was shattered ... and Christ radiated before me" Stein proclaims.[29] All her blinders and interior barriers fall away, and the world of faith gradually unfolds before her.

Yet the near despair of her own heroic struggle to find the Truth teaches Stein the burden of interior darkness. In such an existential crisis, Stein could not awaken her own soul. She had to be renewed by an outside source. "A person can also gradually shrivel up through constant excessive expenditure of power," Stein shares, "and she's got to have new powers supplied to her from an extraneous source so that she rouses again to new life."[30]

Stein explores this theme of inner detachment and the soul's reawakening in her last written work, *The Science of the Cross*, left unfinished upon her arrest and death in the Auschwitz concentration camp in 1942. "There are naturally recognizable signs," she emphasizes, "which indicate that human nature, as it actually is, exists in a state of degeneration. From this stems the

The Soul's Awakening

inability to perceive and respond to facts interiorly in a way that corresponds to their authentic value."[31] Stein is realistic in her assessment of this state of degeneration of human nature. She knows this state can leave us unable to feel genuine emotions or to relate to our fellow man. Our deadened inner state can be attributable to several factors:

> This inability may be grounded in an inborn dull-mindedness (in the literal sense), or in a general indifference developed in the course of a lifetime, or finally, in an insensitivity to certain impressions as a result of repeatedly ignoring them.
>
> What we have often heard and long known "leaves us cold." Added to this, frequently, is an excessive interior preoccupation with one's own personal concerns that refuses to attend to anything else. We know our interior rigidity is inappropriate and it pains us. Knowing that it arises from a psychological law does not help us to overcome it. On the other hand, we rejoice when we can convince ourselves through experience that we are still able to feel deep, genuine joy; and deep, genuine pain also seems to us a grace when compared to our rigid insensitivity.[32]

As Josef Pieper observes in his work on art and contemplation *Only the Lover Sings*: "Man's ability to *see* is in decline ... We do not mean here, of course, the physiological sensitivity of the human eye. We mean the spiritual capacity to perceive the visible reality as it truly is."[33] Such a state of inner blindness, however, is not a permanent condition. There is hope! A soul can be re-awakened from its spiritual stupor. Stein, who has personally experienced such an inner renewal, encourages us:

> In principle, (every individual) has such a center, which can burst forth at any time ... What can help your soul along to its "awakening," that's completely beyond saying. Anything and everything can suddenly strike in the depths, to where nothing was able to make headway before. And if that happens ... the whole abundance of your soul bursts forth in the actuality of living, an actuality which discloses that that living is just now becoming "soul filled."[34]

The soul itself has not been extinguished. Its receptive capacity has been temporarily switched off. Our spiritual capacity can be re-awakened, and light can break through to illuminate our inner darkness. "The love with which I embrace a human being may be sufficient to fill him with new lifepower (*Lebenskraft*) if his own breaks down. Indeed, the mere contact with human beings of more intense aliveness may exert an enlivening effect upon those who are jaded or exhausted."[35] Loving, human contact with another person can reawaken our exhausted or lifeless soul. A simple word of praise, a thoughtful gesture, a kind note, all pour life into our souls. When this life is not accessible from within us, it must be poured upon us from an external source. "Often a single word, a friendly smile, is enough to give a depressed or lonely soul fresh life," St. Thérèse of Lisieux knowingly affirms.[36]

Stein also distinguishes such exterior encouragement from the inner working of God's grace upon the soul. Resting in God, she explains, is an interior emptying in which the soul makes room for God. Such a spiritual state is entirely distinct from the void experienced by an interiorly deadened soul:

> There is a state of resting in God, of complete relaxation of all mental activity, in which you make no plans at all, reach no decision, much less take action, but rather leave everything that's future up to the divine will, "consigning yourself entirely to fate." This state may have befallen me after an experience that exceeded my lifepower, and that has completely consumed my mental lifepower and deprived me of all activeness. Compared to the cessation of activeness from the lack of lifepower, resting in God is something completely new and unique. The former was dead silence. Now its place is taken by the feeling of being safe, of being exempted from all anxiety and responsibility and duty to act. And as I surrender myself to this feeling, new life begins to fill me up, little by little, and impel me—without any voluntary exertion—toward new activation. This reviving infusion appears as an ema-

> nation of a functionality and a power which is not my emanation and which becomes operative within me without my asking for it. The sole prerequisite for such a mental rebirth seems to be a certain receptivity.[37]

Our soul, to live fully, must have a receptive capacity. "If values are going to influence lifepower, the presupposition is that they be *experienced* and that there exist a receptivity for them."[38] A further avenue of receptivity by which we can understand the experience of those around us is the quality of empathy. This interior ability to perceive the experience of another individual is investigated by Stein in her 1917 doctoral dissertation, *On the Problem of Empathy*. She explains that empathy consists of "the perceiving of foreign subjects and their experience."[39] We can only experience our own life from our first-person perspective. Therefore, every other experience which we come to understand is perceived by us through empathy. We are not the other person. But we can better comprehend their experience if we view it through their eyes. "This is how human beings comprehend the psychic life of their fellows," Stein affirms. "Also as believers they comprehend the love, the anger, and the precepts of their God in this way; and God can comprehend people's lives in no other way."[40]

Our ability to comprehend another through empathy depends on our inner receptivity and openness to the other person:

> Were I imprisoned within the boundaries of my individuality, I could not go beyond "the world as it appears to me" ... I cross these boundaries by the help of empathy ... thus empathy as the basis of intersubjective experience becomes the condition of possible knowledge of the existing outer world.[41]

Some individuals have a greater gift of empathy than others. Stein herself was known for her perceptive gift of empathy. We learn on a number of occasions that Stein "had a natural gift of empathy in personal relationships; she felt another's state of mind and knew what to say in encouragement."[42] Whether she was patching up a family argument, assisting soldiers in war time to communicate with home, or identifying with the heavy fate of her Jewish people in the Holocaust, Stein's "spontaneous empathic ability lent Edith herself unusually strong influential powers and harmoniously united intellect and feelings in her own person."[43]

Stein used her gift of empathy, for instance, while serving as a nurse in the First World War. She learned basic questions and answers in nine languages in order to communicate with patients from throughout the Austro-Hungarian Empire. She spoke with these soldiers in their mother tongue and helped them to write letters home, creating a human connection with them despite their natural linguistic boundaries.

She was also a confidante and counselor to the many individuals who sought her listening ear over the years, especially through her written correspondence. Stein speaks from personal experience when she observes: "(The woman) has the faculty to interest herself empathetically in areas of knowledge far from her own concerns and to which she would not pay heed if it were not that a personal interest drew her into contact with them."[44] In a letter from the Cologne cloister to a friend of many years, Stein reiterates that "the formation of an unshakeable bond with all whom life brings in my way, a bond in no way dependent on day-to-day contact, is a significant element in my life. And you can depend on that (tie) even when I do not always reply as promptly as this time."[45]

How then does the gift of empathy impact the creation of the artist and our perception of the artwork? In an analysis of personal formation in "Spirituality of the Christian Woman," a cycle of four lectures given by Stein in Zurich in 1932, she investigates the extent to which the literary characters of Sigrid Undset's Ingunn, Heinrich Ibsen's Nora, and Goethe's Iphigenie are created through the artist's empathic perception. In Sigrid Undset's Ingunn, Stein explains, we meet a character drawn from the artist's raw perception of reality:

The Soul's Awakening

> Hardly anyone could conceive of Sigrid Undset's work as *"l'art pour l'art."* Her creativity is reckless confession. Indeed, one has the impression that she is compelled to express that which presses upon her as brutal reality.[46]

The characters of Nora and Iphigenie, shaped by Ibsen and Goethe, in contrast, have been created through empathic understanding. Both authors are males. They create female literary characters through an empathic understanding of a female's first-hand experience:

> The figure of *Nora* was created by a man who wishes to adopt entirely the woman's perspective, a man who has made the cause of woman and the feminist movement his own. His heroine is chosen from this point of view—but she is precisely chosen and depicted with keenest analysis; she is not invented arbitrarily nor constructed rationalistically. The strength and consequence of her thought and action may be surprising in contrast to what has previously transpired; she may be unusual, yet her action is not an improbable or a completely impossible one.[47]

The character of Nora is true to life. She is true to a life understood empathically by the author, Ibsen. Empathy also plays a role in Goethe's characterization:

> The classical lineaments, the simple grandeur and exalted simplicity of Goethe's most noble female character may appear at first glance to the modern person as most nearly removed from reality. And idealism is certainly under consideration here; but again, this is no construction of fantasy but rather an idealized image which is envisioned, experienced, and empathized from life itself.[48]

A glance upon the sculptor Michelangelo's artwork, furthermore, reveals the infusion of his artistic gift with empathy. Michelangelo's *Pietà* depicts the sublime suffering of the Blessed Mother, cradling her Son taken down from the Cross.[49] Our Lady's face is a study in accepted agony. Michelangelo did not suffer the agony of Mary; he comprehends Our Lady's sorrow by standing in Our Lady's place and viewing the Crucifixion from her perspective. He then crafts in marble the emotion which he has experienced empathically. We, the art-receiver, are given access to a deeper understanding of Our Lady's experience through Michelangelo's gift of perception. A creative artist's "gift of empathy," Stein concludes, "may inspire or demand this particular kind of expression, and they may then be induced to reproduce this empathetic experience in their work."[50]

Empathy also plays a vital role in the appreciation of the created work by the art receiver. Stein draws upon the character of Achilles from Homer's *Illiad* to explain:

> The rancor of Achilles is no real rancor: It does not really arise out of the depths of the essence, and that which unfolds itself is no real essence. In short, Achilles is no *ousia*, no independently and authentically existing being. Achilles, and with him the entire "world" into which he has been placed, are sustained by the spirit of the poet (or of the empathetic reader).[51]

The world of poetic imagination is suspended, held in existence, through both the empathy of the artist and the art receiver.

Finally, an objectifying clarification must take place for the understanding gained through empathy to be complete. Since, through empathy, "I am at the subject of the content in the original subject's place," I must then return to my own two feet, to a perspective from which "the content again face(s) me as object."[52] In a theatrical setting, for example, I attend a drama and willingly enter the imaginary world presented. I imbibe the emotions of the characters on the stage, but these are not my firsthand emotions. "While I am living in the other's joy, I do not feel primordial joy. It does not issue live from my "I," Stein explains.[53] I then return to reality, to my own personal existence, when the curtain closes. What I have experienced from the other's perspective now informs my understanding with deeper insight.

It is possible, however, that we fail to progress to this final clarification. Too often, and all-too possibly, the deception of "borrowed embers" takes place.[54] We may "take feelings 'acquired by reading' to be our own," Stein warns, "for instance, the young girl thinks she feels Juliet's love."[55] The reader, although captivated by the literary experience, is *not* Juliet of Shakespeare's drama. We may have entered the experience of the character's star-crossed love; however, we must return to our own existence, seeing Juliet outside of ourselves, next to us, apart from us. If we lack the wherewithal to achieve this clarification, the objectification will, Stein assures us, occur eventually. "This flame will go out of its own accord, as soon as the embers die out. Because a primordial valuing is lacking as a foundation, we also have 'non-genuineness' here."[56]

We see the tendency to "non-genuine" living in an unreal existence in the modern technology milieu. Many young girls, for example, may seek an emotional oneness with social media idols. They project themselves into the experience of another, losing their own identity in the process. They begin to think perhaps they *are* the influencing glamour girl or the protagonist of the music video. They dress, think, and speak like another person, losing their genuine personality and taking on the identity of another. Many young boys, likewise, seek to become the hero or villain of the video warfare game, often without a distinction from actual reality. In such virtual immersion, the connection to the real world becomes tenuous and blurred. The parameters of real life become indistinct from the borrowed life. As one technology addiction expert recounts, regarding a young man immersed in video gaming:

> As he walked into my office, he looked dazed and disoriented ... and terrified.
> ... I asked him if he knew where he was; he didn't answer. He just kept nervously blinking and looking around, his head in perpetual motion.
> "Dan, do you know where you are?" I asked once again.
> Again, no answer.

> ... Then, finally, he looked straight at me and stammered in a tone of genuine confusion: "Are ... are ... we still in the game?"[57]

To clarify reality, we close the book, the curtain falls on the play, but how do we clarify the boundary between virtual and actual reality? Many technology addiction programs emphasize real world experiences such as hiking in nature, fishing, horseback riding, and team building challenges, to re-ground young people who have lost their connection to their identity and the real world. The ability to feel first-hand emotion, and to take first-hand responsibility for our actions, comes from the necessary distinction between ourselves and the borrowed reality we have inhabited temporarily.

Stein became more aware of the needs and experiences of others through empathy. We must likewise take what we comprehend through empathy, this bridge to another person, and become more understanding, more patient, more kind, more solicitous to the needs of our neighbor. Each person becomes accessible, and our life is enriched through our deeper understanding of the lives around us. We can then contribute to the life of the community and its members, reaching out to the other whose experience we have understood more fully. We think of the communion of saints, of the Church militant on earth, of the Church suffering in Purgatory. Our souls are created to touch one another. In Charles Dickens' profound story of redemption, *A Christmas Carol*, the spirit of Jacob Marley exhorts Ebenezer Scrooge: "My spirit never walked beyond our counting house—mark me!—in life my spirit never roved beyond the narrow limits of our money-changing hole."[58] Because Marley never glanced upon his fellow man in life, his ghost is condemned to walk the earth repenting of his isolated indifference:

> It is required of every man ... that the spirit within him should walk abroad among his fellow-men, and travel far and wide ... Mankind was my business. The common welfare was my business; charity, mercy, forbearance, and

> benevolence, were all my business. The dealings of my trade were but a drop of water in the comprehensive ocean of my business ... Why did I walk through crowds of fellow-beings with my eyes turned down, and never raise them to that blessed Star which led the Wise Men to a poor abode! Were there no poor homes to which its light would have conducted *me*![59]

Each soul touches another. Our lives are a gift for others. As we follow His prompting, we touch the world with His love, bringing His beauty to the hearts of all those He places in our path.

Beauty and the Human Spirit

As our souls respond to beauty, awakening to the objective value before us, the artistic work has a unique capacity to touch our spirit. Why is this? The words in a poem or the sounds in a melody, Stein explains, convey to us a glimpse of the fullness of meaning which the artist has perceived and presented to us through the artwork. As she affirms in *The Science of the Cross*, every genuine artwork "comes from that infinite fullness of meaning"[60] and speaks of this infinite fullness to us in finite, tangible form. This fullness of meaning then "demands to gain life in a human soul," and it comes to life in the souls of both the artist and the art-receiver.[61] Not only do we encounter the spirit of the artist through the artwork, but, even more powerfully, we encounter the origin of the beauty which inspired the work itself. Regarding the musical arts, for instance, Stein explains:

> A melody is not a mere sequence of sounds sensorially experienced. We hear in it the singing of a human soul—in jubilation or mourning, in a placid or angry mood. We understand the "language" of this melody. It touches and moves our soul; we meet in it a life that is akin to our own.[62]

The language of the arts is, therefore, a language which the soul understands. Our soul responds to the triumph imbued in the strain of music, to the heroism of the literary character, or the tranquility of the pastoral landscape. Through his work, the artist serves as an intermediary between us and the pure idea behind the work:

> We understand this expression even without paying attention to the artist whose mediatorship has made it possible for us to gain access to it. In this way we may also understand and appreciate the meaning of a poem without paying attention to the personal characteristics of the handwriting of the poet.[63]

The encounter with the pure idea expressed through music, Stein explains, is an experience which moves from the musical notes themselves to the complete musical expression which transmits a fullness of meaning to the listener. For Stein, "the meaning of a melody ... molds a series of sounds or tones so that they become a unified 'tone-structure,'" in which "each individual sound or tone is itself a meaningful structure that has the possibility of entering into a higher unity of meaning."[64] These tones can then be "actualized as sound in space and time by vibration produced by the human voice or by musical instruments"[65] whereby, she explains, the idea behind the music is formed into a created sound. The pure idea is expressed as something we can hear and comprehend. The music brings our soul alive when the profound and intangible idea behind it, triumph, despair, love, sacrifice, jubilation, is experienced by the listener through actual sound. Then, Stein explains, "the *matter* which presents itself for such an entering is the *life* of the soul, its *spiritual* life."[66] When this occurs, she concludes, "the life filled with meaning ... is superabundant, diffusive life. It has a form of being which we call *spiritual*."[67] In listening to Edward Elgar's "Lux Aeterna" or Pietro Mascagni's "Cavalleria Rusticana: Intermezzo," superabundant life enters the soul. We encounter the original, pure idea which the musical score seeks to communicate. The notes themselves serve to express the entirety of the eternal beauty experienced by the artist and expressed to us in sound. In its expression of this fullness of meaning, music can therefore transmit life to us and renew our soul.

The artwork has the profound ability to place the soul in relation to the pure idea, or archetype, which the work faithfully represents. Stein affirms that "artistic truth denotes congruity of the work of art with a pure idea."[68] Through the created work, then, we are able to ascend "from the finite and conditioned to the infinite and unconditioned author and archetype of everything finite and conditioned."[69] This passing from the finite to the infinite through the created work gives to the work an awesome dignity. "The entire structure of created existents ('that which is') turns into an image of the Triune Deity."[70] All created matter in this sense reveals the uncreated Source of Being. "For," as the Book of Wisdom proclaims, "from the greatness and the beauty of created things comes a corresponding perception of their Creator" (Wisdom 18:8).

The archetype manifested through the artwork provides a glimmer of the divine archetype which is its ultimate origin, and through the artwork the veil is lifted. Stein explains this revelatory nature of the artwork itself:

> It is simultaneously *image* (Bild) in which something is presented and *structure* (Gebilde) as something formed into a complete and all-encompassing little world of its own. Every genuine work of art is in addition a *symbol* (Sinnbild) whether or not this is its creator's intention, be he naturalist or symbolist.
>
> It is a symbol: that is, it comes from that infinite fullness of *meaning* (Sinn) into which every bit of human knowledge is projected to grasp something positive and speak of it. It does so in such a manner, in fact, that it mysteriously suggests the whole fullness of meaning, which for all human knowledge is inexhaustible.[71]

The artwork points us to the whole fullness of meaning because this fullness is its origin. For this reason, Stein concludes, "All genuine art is revelation and all artistic creation is sacred service."[72] Every genuine artwork, in which the work of art faithfully corresponds to the pure idea which is its origin, reveals to us the entire fullness of meaning which is behind all creation. The role of the artist then becomes a sacred task, to reveal to us the divine archetype mysteriously suggested by its presentation in tangible image form.

Because genuine art reveals its divine origin, it follows that the artwork must directly affect our interior state. Our encounter with the infinite fullness of meaning, an encounter produced by the artwork, must leave us changed, interiorly transformed. In fact, Stein warns, "there is a danger, in an artistic inclination, and not only when the artist lacks an understanding of the sacredness of his task. The danger lies in the possibility that in constructing the image, the artist proceeds as though there were no further responsibility than producing it."[73]

What responsibility does the artwork demand of us? Fundamental to Stein's vision of beauty, art, and sanctity, is the assertion that both the artist and the art-receiver are responsible for a proper personal response to the encounter with the divine archetype revealed by the artwork. This critical responsibility is delineated by Stein, in *The Science of the Cross*, through the example of an artistic depiction of the Cross:

> There will scarcely be a believing artist who has not felt compelled to portray Christ on the cross or carrying the cross. But the Crucified One demands from the artist more than a mere portrayal of the image. He demands that the artist, just as every other person, follow him: that he both make himself and allow himself to be made into an image of the one who carries the cross and is crucified.[74]

It is probable that St. John's famous sketch of the Crucifixion was in Stein's mind in this regard. We know of her familiarity with the work, which she mentions in a letter to a fellow Carmelite detailing her own attempts at drawing a copy of John's sketch as she was writing *The Science of the Cross*:

> I tried to make a copy of the sketch our Holy Father John made on a piece of paper about 5 cm. in size, after the vision he had of the Crucified at the Monastery of the Incarnation. The reproduction of it in P. Bruno's book is not exactly sharp, and I am anything but an artist. But I made it with great reverence and love, and think that Your Reverence will get at least a little idea of it.[75]

As Stein produces her artistic copy of St. John's sketch of the Crucifixion, she is aware that more is demanded of the artist than the mere portrayal of the image. More is also demanded of the art-receiver than mere aesthetic admiration. Because the artwork provides a window to the fullness of meaning, the work requires our internal response to that profound meaning which it reveals:

> Expressing the image externally can be a hindrance to doing so internally, but by no means must this be so; actually, it can serve the process of interior transformation because only with the production of the external expression will the inner image be fully formed and interiorly adopted. In this manner, when no obstacle is placed in its path, it becomes an interior representation that urges the artist to effectively reproduce it in action, that is, by way of imitation, externally.[76]

St. John of the Cross, whose artistic creation Stein analyzes in depth, responded interiorly to his encounter with the One who carries the Cross. "Yes," she affirms, "the external image, one's own artistic creation, can always serve to spur one on to transform oneself interiorly according to its meaning".[77] St. John of the Cross's response to this fullness of meaning is a life of holiness, an embrace of the Cross in actual lived experience:

> His love of the image of the Cross shows how deeply he loved Christ Crucified, whose picture gave his small house at Duruelo its characteristic atmosphere ... It may be assumed that the first Discalced Carmelite who had once been an apprentice of image carvers and painters

> had himself made these Crosses to adorn his tiny monastery ... He wanted to lead himself and others to union by the image of the Cross.[78]

In St. John's response of holiness, Stein affirms, "we are not dealing merely with a theory ... but a living, real, and effective truth."[79] St. John's artistic expression reveals a lived and intimate understanding, a *science* of the Cross.:

> One feels how, for the saint, the veils are raised and everything becomes transparent for the enlightenment of the mysterious commerce between God and the soul. What appears to the unenlightened gaze of the ordinary reader as mere external occurrence, St. John *reads* as though it self-evidently is an expression of a mystical happening.[80]

Our comprehension of the artwork must then pass from an external, outward appreciation to an embrace of the deeper reality which the artwork reveals. "For if," as St. John of the Cross maintains, "I surrender to the delight I have in the stimulants, that which serves as a support for my imperfection will become a hindrance ... just as attachment and inclination for anything else."[81] The delight which the artwork evokes calls us to recognize and respond to the deeper value which it heralds. Stein reiterates this interplay between the gladness which the artwork evokes in me and the divine origin to which it points:

> When I surrender myself wholeheartedly to the beauty beheld, then the gladness recedes for me—the fully alive, felt aesthetic gladness without which such a surrender isn't possible. On the other hand, if I surrender myself consciously to the gladness, and if it becomes the most important thing for me, then the value I'm glad about slips away from me, in its own distinctive manner.[82]

The glimmer of divine beauty revealed through the artwork beckons to my soul through the mysterious melody of the musical score, the wash of colors across the canvas, the outline of the cathedral arches against the skyline. But I don't stay focused on the melody, colors, or cathedral. I am called to go deeper. I move through them to the eternal beauty they manifest. I encounter God Himself through these images and grasp echoes of His Divine Being. In his *Letter to Artists*, Pope St. John Paul II celebrates this power of the artwork "to affirm that true beauty which, as a glimmer of the Spirit of God, will transfigure matter, opening the human soul to the sense of the eternal."[83] The result of our encounter with such an artwork is our interior awakening. We leave the encounter with the artwork changed. We become more fully alive to ourselves, to those around us, and to the Divine Being whose splendor we have encountered through His revelation in created image.

The power of the artwork to awaken our soul through a revelatory encounter with the divine archetype is especially important when our inner receptivity has fallen dormant within us. An individual cannot bring an ability or predisposition alive within himself which he does not possess. However, such abilities sometimes lie dormant within us through lack of exposure to artistic values, or the opportunity to encounter them. Our spiritual capacity then lies inactive, to the detriment of our own development and the development of those around us whose lives we are in turn meant to impact. When this is true, the artwork presents to me the lifepower which can inspire me and transform my inner life. When we encounter beauty through the artwork, we are enlivened:

> The impression we obtain from a figure of history or fiction can "fire us up" and invigorate us just like that of someone living ... The beauty of a figure that I behold ignites in me the enthusiasm that spurs me to artistic creation. The hero of an epic poem fills me with admiration, and out of that admiration the urge wells up to emulate him. In both cases the experienced values are not only motives that prescribe the direction of my deed, but at the same time they furnish the propellant powers that it requires.[84]

The artwork, therefore, both motivates my new action and provides for me the power which I need in order act. For Stein, the infinite fullness of meaning revealed by the artwork is charged with potential energy, like a piece of food or firewood. The encounter of the human spirit with this potential energy converts it into kinetic, active, power within us. "Although the artwork (to which Stein's thought turns among other things when she evokes the impersonal products created by the spirit) is non-living, therefore in itself unable to generate the propulsive force toward a goal, its meaning is 'charged with strength' (with *potential energy*) and is discharged upon entering again into living connection with a spiritual person."[85] Exposure to beauty is life-giving. Beauty can "convey new propellant powers to our mental life."[86] When beauty conveys such new power to the soul, it is regarded by Stein as "'life-contributing.'"[87]

Has a work of literature ever reinvigorated our soul? Has a piece of classical music renewed our spirit? In her own life, Stein frequently and intentionally drew upon such "propellant powers" from artistic sources, transforming this lifegiving power into efficacious action. Under the strenuous burden of her teaching responsibilities and academic work, she sought renewed strength, for example, from the works of Shakespeare:

> If anything could sadden (my mother) in those days, it was the enormous workload I was carrying. Upon coming home from school, I put all my school matters aside and took up my doctoral work. The family got to see me at the evening meal; but as soon as it was over, I withdrew again. Only at about ten at night would I begin preparing the following day's classes. If, while doing so, I became so fatigued that I could no longer grasp anything, I would read a bit of Shakespeare. That so renewed my vitality that I was able to begin again.[88]

The spark of the human spirit conveyed in a few lines from the master playwright reinvigorated Stein's spirit and her mental vitality.

Stein also recounts an incident which took place while she was studying at the University of Breslau, in which a musical score lifted her from profound discouragement and rekindled her hope:

> It was probably the summer of 1912 when I read the controversial novel, *Helmut Harringa*. Portraying student life, it portrayed in frighteningly vivid color the deplorable conditions in the fraternities with their senseless drinking requirements and the consequent moral aberrations. I was filled with such aversion that it took weeks before I recovered from it. I had lost all confidence in the persons with whom I associated daily; I went about as one unbearably burdened; and I was beyond finding enjoyment in anything at all. What cured me of this depression is highly significant. That year a great Bach Festival was given in Breslau. Bach was my favorite, so naturally I had a ticket for each of the performances: an organ concert; chamber music; and a gala evening of orchestral and vocal music. I no longer recall which oratorio was being presented that evening. I only know that Luther's defiant hymn "A Mighty Fortress" was included. I had always liked singing it in our school devotions. When, in stirring battle cry, the verse was sung:
> "And though this world with devils filled
> Should threaten to undo us
> We will not fear,
> ... truth will triumph through us"
> my pessimistic outlook vanished completely. True, the world might be evil; but if the small group of friends in whom I had confidence and I strove with all our might, we should certainly have done with all "devils."[89]

Stein also renewed her strength by reading ancient Greek literature when she served as a nurse in a hospital for infectious diseases during the First World War. "I went along the rows and satisfied myself about the condition of the critically ill," she relates. "When bedtime came for the patients, and nothing particular had to be done, I sat at the small prescription desk and wrote letters or read. I had brought only two books to Weisskirchen: Husserl's *Ideen* and Homer."[90]

True to her belief in the renewing power of beauty, Stein also sought out liturgical beauty to replenish her soul during her strenuous years as a Catholic professional in the secular world. In the years following her conversion, during her teaching, writing, and lecturing throughout Germany, Stein made a point of traveling each year to the abbey town of Beuron to participate in the beautiful Holy Week liturgies offered there. Although these trips involved considerable extra time and travel in an already demanding schedule, Stein especially treasured the unique aesthetic and spiritual richness which Beuron offered. She drew inner strength and renewal from the sacred music, art, and liturgical offerings of the Benedictine Abbey. In his biography of Stein written for her canonization, Fr. Giovanni della Croce, OCD, notes:

> Not far from Speyer, near to Freiburg, is the great Benedictine Abbey of Beuron, an important center for liturgical form, as well as music, and sacred art, celebrated for the renewal of Gregorian chant with the translation of the ancient texts into German. Having made a first visit to Beuron, Edith returned there attracted by the splendid liturgical functions.[91]

Stein refers to these treasured encounters with beauty in her autobiographical account, "How I Came to the Cologne Carmel," observing: "On Thursday of Passion Week (1933), I traveled to Beuron. Since 1928 I had spent that week and the Easter holiday there each year and had quietly held my own private retreat."[92] In a letter written from Beuron on Palm Sunday of 1932, Stein reveals the interior nourishment which these visits provided her soul:

> I have often reflected whether my coming here so frequently is justifiable. But after all, one has to provide one's inner life with the nourishment it needs, especially

when at other times we are required to give a great deal to others. Obviously, one cannot discuss this with persons who are oriented purely to material matters, and who have no sense for the values of spirit or soul.[93]

With her entrance into Carmel, Stein's aesthetic preference for high liturgical celebration was joyfully sacrificed for the simpler aesthetic of her new religious order. "Of course, we have nothing to offer you," she notes in a letter written shortly after her entrance, "no beautiful liturgy at all, or the like. Only our joyful poverty and our peace."[94] The delight which Stein experienced, therefore, when her community participated in a sung mass on her name-day in honor of St. Benedict, is especially touching:

> You asked about my name-patron. Of course it is holy Father Benedict. He adopted me and gave me the rights of home in his Order, even though I was not even an Oblate since I always had the Mount of Carmel before my eyes. Because of that my Carmelite Mother gave me the pleasure that yesterday—at the public celebration of our feast day (of St. Benedict)—we were allowed to sing a choral High Mass. That is something most extraordinary. Usually we remain very silent behind the grate, and visiting choirs sing the high Masses in our church. Eleven years ago, when that kind of dearth existed for a longer period, our Sisters learned (to sing) several high Masses under P. Ballman, OSB (Abbey of Maria Laach). So now the choral books were taken out; a very capable chaplain from St. George's helped with the practice and accompanied us; for support he brought six choir boys as cantors for the parts of the Common. Everyone was satisfied with the High Mass and the eight (Sister) singers were happy.[95]

Given Stein's deep appreciation of liturgical beauty, it is fitting that her superiors asked her to compose the texts for the *Mass and Office in Honor of Our Lady Queen of Peace*, submitted to the Vatican for the approval of a First Class Feast for Carmel in honor of Our Lady, *Regina Pacis*.[96] On a private visit to Pope St. John Paul II, in the Papal Apartments, I gave the Holy Pontiff a personal copy of Stein's liturgical texts. Perhaps one day the

Mass in Honor of Our Lady Queen of Peace can be celebrated in honor of St. Edith Stein being named a Doctor of the Universal Church.

The Revival of the Community

Stein expands her analysis of the arts to address the relationship between the artist, the artwork, and the community. A civilization, she explains, has "created out of itself an inexhaustible fountain, as it were, from which it can always draw new powers."[97] But we can let these cultural fountains fall dormant. If this happens, the propellant powers of a civilization are not extinguished, but the soul's capacity to respond to this beauty is temporarily switched off. These works then "exist without deploying any live efficacy … In such cases you talk about an 'extinct civilization.'"[98] The life-giving power of the civilization, of a cultural patrimony, is efficacious to the extent that our spiritual capacity can respond to its value. The works themselves have an inextinguishable life within; we must only reactivate our ability to receive their lifepower. In fact, we can draw anew from this "inexhaustible fountain" at any time:

> A branch of civilization can "wither away" while the nation to which it owes its existence lives on, and not only when the nation itself perishes. Then truly it's not the civilization that's dead—its life endures perpetually. Rather, it's the souls upon whom the civilization should be bestowing life. Certain layers of their life are switched off. That the civilization isn't dead is shown by the fact that it can undergo a "renaissance" at any time. It needs only to be discovered anew in order to become operative and bestow power.[99]

The artwork is not dead, the sacred music is not dead, the cathedral is not dead, we are! When the *Cathedral Notre Dame de Paris* burned, the world mourned the loss of a living, breathing part of our lives. Our collective grief was surprising to us.

Why did we feel the loss of a building so deeply? Modern man had assumed that the structure had long been relegated to the status of a cultural artifact. In actuality, the cathedral was a source of lifepower for the community in ways we did not perceive. In fact, the lifepower of a *Notre Dame* cannot be extinguished. Our souls must be awakened to respond to this power anew.

The artist therefore has a unique role in assisting "the revival of a community by the world of values."[100] The souls of the individuals who comprise the community can be re-awakened to genuine soul-filled living. Of importance here is Stein's definition of the contrast between a community and an association. The essential distinction between these two social formations is the relationship between the people within them. In an association "one person approaches another as *subject* to *object*, examines her, deals with her methodically on the basis of the knowledge obtained, and coaxes the intended reactions out of her."[101] In a community, conversely, "a subject accepts the other *as a subject* and does not confront him but rather *lives with him* and is determined by the stirrings of his life."[102] Isolation and impersonal transactions are the earmarks of the association, while human connection and inter-personal relationships are affirmed through community. "In the association, everyone is absolutely alone, a 'windowless monad.' In the community, solidarity prevails."[103]

In the community, the artist has a vital role. The image which an artist creates opens a bridge between subjects and communicates values from one person to the other. Only by passing the values on to the next member of the community can the ideas behind each artwork touch the souls of those around us:

> Just think, how few of our leading minds ... have approached the graphic arts of antiquity, and have filled themselves with its mind, and how little of that has penetrated into the souls of the German people; how the upper layers of society in Germany in the seventeenth and eighteenth century were pervaded by French cultural

> influences while the core of the nation was essentially untouched by it; how nearly the whole trend of our modern art remains misunderstood and ineffective amidst the life of the national community. So it's important, that those who possess the eyes open to the world of values be living as members of the community, in live interaction with its other components. Whoever locks himself up inside himself, whoever won't let the abundance of his inner life become efficacious outwardly, can't be considered an organ of the community and doesn't open up access for it to the sources from which it can be supplied with propellant powers.[104]

And what if we remain closed within ourselves? An individual life is conceivable, Stein points out, "that doesn't pay off for any community either in works or in determining influence: a personality, for example, who pursues scientific research without letting anyone participate in it, or who builds up a new ability of aesthetic enjoyment in herself without letting anything of it become outwardly noticeable so that it could 'offer an example' in the community."[105] Such isolation shares no life-giving fruit with others. A life-giving effect occurs, however, when those who have been touched by a profound encounter with beauty share this source of lifepower with others:

> If for the time being we leave aside the works of civilization, and if we consider the scenery as a bearer of aesthetic value, then we find a striking example for making intuitable for ourselves the phenomenon that we have in view: the fact that the beauty of the alpine world remained entirely concealed well into the eighteenth century. We may take in hand Livy's famous description of Hannibal's crossing of the Alps or Haller's elaborate poem. We find there a lot about the horrors and dangers of the mountains, and a good deal about the peculiarities of the land and its inhabitants, but nary a word about aesthetic attractions. What today is a self-evident possession of the world of European civilization collectively was

> gained for it by single personalities. (We can name their names: Rousseau, Goethe, and others).[106]

Individuals such as Rousseau and Goethe perceived aesthetic value in the alpine world and communicated that value to the community through their works. Such a formative influence upon the civilization is possible when the perceiving individual lives in interaction with the community itself. "Insofar as (a person's life) precipitates in objective 'works,'" Stein concludes, "it can become the common possession of the nation or of humanity, or it can exert influence upon the mind of one community or another and thereby upon the development of its character and the further course of its life."[107] We could call this phenomenon the George Bailey effect, captured so poignantly by director Frank Capra in his 1946 film *It's a Wonderful Life*. By removing the presence of George from the life of Bedford Falls, Capra reveals Stein's thesis that one individual can exert an irreplaceable influence upon the entire life of a community.

We think here of the pervasive impact which the life and talents of Sir Christopher Wren poured forth on the city of London and the cultural revival of the British architectural landscape. Wren's London emerged after the Great Fire of 1666 destroyed much of the medieval cityscape. His works became what Stein would term "the common possession of the nation."[108] One artistic soul, in relationship with the community, can affect the entire course of its life. Fittingly, Wren's tombstone in St. Paul's Cathedral, translated from the Latin, reads: "Underneath lies buried Christopher Wren, the builder of this church and city; who lived beyond the age of ninety years, not for himself, but for the public good. If you seek his memorial, look about you."[109]

In her analysis of the individual's ability to influence the community, and our duty to live in relation to the human beings around us, sharing our life with them as persons and not treating them as objects, Stein prophetically anticipates the lethal social architecture of National Socialism. The manipulation of subjects as objects in an association, which is the hallmark of the dehumanizing Nazi ideology, stands in stark contrast to a respect for the individual in a community as a vital element in the authentic development of its members. As the editor to *Philosophy of Psychology and the Humanities* notes:

> This passage, written about 1919, is among those that (whether rightly or wrongly) have earned Stein the reputation of having prophetically foreseen the process through which National Socialists would achieve political power in Germany. Ironically, while Nazi ideology was talking the talk ... characteristic of community, Stein's analysis indicates that Nazi practices exemplified the disingenuous rhetoric of "association men and women."[110]

Due to the vital, life-giving nature of his task, therefore, a series of responsibilities falls upon the artist. He must live as an authentic member of the community in order that his receptivity to ideas and creative expression may be efficaciously shared with others. Furthermore, he must have "an understanding of the sacredness of his task."[111] Stein recognizes the possibility that man's fallen nature can affect his creative art:

> The decay of man's dominion is seen when we consider his relationship to the natural riches of the earth: instead of a reverential joy in the created world, instead of a desire to preserve and develop it, man seeks to exploit it greedily to the point of destruction or to senseless acquisition without understanding how to profit from it or how to enjoy it. Related to this is the debasement of creative art through the violent distortion and caricature of natural images.[112]

Contrary to such debased distortion, the faithful revelation of the archetype through the artwork leads us to its divine origin, making the artist's task truly sacred.

Fidelity in bringing forth the idea behind the artwork is, for Stein, the most fundamental aspect of artistic creation. The artist's task, then, is one of elucidation as much as of creation. In the artistic process the artist perceives the pure idea or meaningful structure behind the artwork, and he crafts the artwork to faithfully express this idea. The creation of the artwork, therefore, is a process of receiving the archetype and presenting it faithfully in created form. "If we now examine more closely what happens on the part of the artist," Stein explains, "we find ... that the 'emergence' of the 'idea' is more in the nature of receiving than of creation."[113] In other words, the artist calls forth the work to correspond with the idea he has perceived. Stein clarifies, "The human intellect does not call *ideas* into *Dasein* (existence); it calls works into *Dasein* (existence) which it fashions."[114] The artist comprehends the idea behind the artwork and then re-creates the idea as closely and faithfully as possible in material form. As Stein explains, "meaningful structures are not created but merely re-created or copied by human beings. They have an *ideal* or *essential* being of their own, and there corresponds to them a proportionate *matter* which is formed by them and by means of which they are 'actualized.'"[115] Genuine art, for Stein, is thus an artwork which corresponds faithfully to the pure idea which it reveals.

Furthermore, the process of crafting the artwork clarifies more fully the artist's understanding of the idea itself. The archetype behind the artwork is not immediately and perfectly represented through the artwork. These ideas "do not manifest themselves immediately in full clarity and intelligibility but rather in a veiled and indistinct manner," such that "the clarification takes place step by step during and concomitantly with the execution of the work"[116] The artist more fully understands the idea behind the artwork as he crafts it. An actor will tell you that he comes to comprehend the character he interprets more fully through dramatization. Shades of personality, and hidden depths of meaning in the spoken words of the character, are revealed and unveiled through the actor's rehearsal and finally through his live performance. An author will likewise tell you that his literary character comes to clarity through the process of creation on the page. The motivations and reactions of the character might even be unpredictable to the author, who waits, in a sense, to see how the characters will reveal themselves. The revelation of the archetype in the material artwork is an unfolding and unveiling.

Stein often explains this interplay between the artist's comprehension of the idea and its revelation in material form, through a sculptor and his block of marble. Within the marble under the artist's chisel, the idea and its manifestation in tangible form interact to become one artistic formation:

> The sculptor may first have an "idea" and then seek for suitable "material." But it may also happen that the sculptor receives the first "inspiration" at the sight of a block of marble which suggests certain possibilities of artistic formation. Though the block of marble is not yet the work, it is nevertheless an essential part of the work. The artistic "plan" or "design" owes not only its existence to the block of marble. Even the content of this plan may be co-determined by the block of marble.[117]

The great sculptor Michelangelo's approach to his artistic creations often occurred as Stein describes. He insisted that the artwork was within the marble, and his master craft was to chip away the excess and extricate the figure from the stone. Michelangelo's artistic genius revealed the figure imprisoned in the marble, freeing his masterpiece from the extraneous material.

The artist works to intellectually grasp the idea behind the artwork, the archetype, and then uses his skill to transform the idea as closely as possible into tangible form. The idea itself is not the artwork. The tangible form allows the idea to emerge for our comprehension. Stein further elucidates the interplay between artwork and idea through the literary artist's relationship to a fictional character:

> The formal structures which artists mold have their own nature, a nature which "unfolds" before their very eyes. They "watch" them, observing how they "behave" in this

> or that particular situation; they have no dictatorial power over them ... Such poetic characters *are*, however, not *pure forms* because their structure includes some *material elements* by means of which they take hold of the form and make it intelligible to others. In the case of poetry the chief (though not the only) material element is language.[118]

The completed artwork is "true," Stein asserts, "when it *is* what it *ought* to be."[119] This truthfulness stems entirely from correspondence with the pure idea, not correspondence with the artist's intention:

> This "ought" has a twofold meaning. It may indicate that the work of art corresponds to the intention of the artist, or that it corresponds to the pure idea. The work is not a genuine or true work of art if—though the work expresses the intention of the artist—the idea which the artist has fashioned in his or her mind deviates from the pure idea.[120]

The artist must therefore remain faithful to the pure idea, re-creating it as closely as possible in material form. Thus Stein emphasizes that "for a 'genuine' or 'true' work of art it is of the utmost importance that nothing be done aimlessly or capriciously lest the inner organic laws of the formal structure be disturbed by any arbitrary additions, omissions, or distortions."[121] To the extent that the artwork is a faithful expression of the pure idea upon which it is based, it is genuine. The more closely the artwork resembles its archetype, the more of a true masterpiece it becomes.

Stein is also aware of the possibility of remaining on the surface in the aesthetic enjoyment of the artwork. The exterior beauty of the artwork can be esteemed to the neglect of the deeper eternal beauty which the artwork makes manifest. This neglect hinders the inner response in each of our souls called for by the fullest meaning of the artwork. In this way works of art, even of purely religious subjects, "'may be occasions of great vanity and vain joy,' if men 'consider the rarity and artistic value of a picture rather than what it represents.'"[122]

Finally, in its revelation of the essential truth of the pure idea upon which it is based, the artwork can "aid us in our understanding of reality and real existence."[123] The portrait or literary depiction, for instance, can reveal a profound truth about the person, because it corresponds to the pure idea, or essential truth, of the person depicted. The individual may have had aspects of his or her personality never fulfilled in their actual life. The painting reveals the essential traits of the person, corresponding to their perfect archetype. The artistic depiction can therefore show us the potential possessed by that individual but perhaps never fully realized historically.

What does this mean? For Stein, the truth presented in the artwork can bring us closer to the essence of the person than historical representation might express. In a portrait, we meet Napoleon's immense potential, for instance, from which he may have fallen short. We meet the pure idea of Napoleon, corresponding to his essence:

> We may be sure, for example, that the life of the historical Napoleon was not a pure realization of what he ought to have been. Now it is the task of the historian to report what Napoleon actually did and how he behaved in reality. But the historian would fulfill this task in an imperfect manner if the image of Napoleon showed none of the luster of that *pure idea* to which Napoleon ought to have corresponded. For what each human being ought to be—i.e., his or her "personal destiny"—pertains to the essence. This is why the artist, who penetrates through the purely external and factual to the primordial archetype (*Urbild*), can present more of the truth than the historian who remains within the limited circumference of external data. The work of the artist who succeeds in depicting the true *Urbild* and at the same time remaining within the bounds of tradition will be truer even in the

sense of historical truth than the work of a historian who does not penetrate beyond the surface of external facts.[124]

The portrait painter, therefore, has a mighty power. He can reveal a depth of the essence of Napoleon, the "luster of the *pure idea* to which Napoleon ought to have corresponded."[125] The artwork reveals a flash of greatness in the look of the eye, an expression of determination and valor in his bearing, which the historical man may or may not have fulfilled. In this way the artistic depiction is, for Stein, more authentic than the "truth of the historian who remains within the limited circumference of external data."[126]

Stein's understanding of the authentic artwork encapsulates her vision of the human person. From all eternity God envisions our fullness, and He calls this forth in us throughout our lives. We spend our lives corresponding, to a greater or lesser extent, to the pure idea that God has conceived of us from all eternity. Before He formed us in the womb, He knew every aspect of our being. He sees all that we can become. He knows us as fully Michael, or fully Maria, or fully Anne, or Paul, or John, in our eternal calling and personhood. Just like the genuine artwork, when we correspond in our actual lives as perfectly as possible to all that God envisions, we become a masterpiece of the Divine Artist.

Notes

1. Stein, *Philosophy of Psychology*, 159.
2. "Editor's Introduction" and "Preface," in *Philosophy of Psychology*, xi, x.
3. "Editor's Introduction" in *Philosophy of Psychology*, xxii.
4. Stein, *Philosophy of Psychology*, 159.
5. Stein, *Philosophy of Psychology*, 159, italics added.
6. Editor's note, *Philosophy of Psychology*, 159.
7. Stein, *Philosophy of Psychology*, 162.
8. Stein, *Philosophy of Psychology*, 162.
9. Stein, *Philosophy of Psychology*, 159.
10. Stein, *Philosophy of Psychology*, 162.
11. Stein, *Philosophy of Psychology*, 159.
12. Stein, *Philosophy of Psychology*, 228.
13. Stein, *Philosophy of Psychology*, 228.
14. Stein, *Philosophy of Psychology*, 231.
15. Stein, *Philosophy of Psychology*, 230.
16. Stein, *Philosophy of Psychology*, 234.
17. Stein, *Philosophy of Psychology*, 235.
18. Stein, *Philosophy of Psychology*, 235
19. Stein, *Philosophy of Psychology*, 235.
20. Blessed Carlo Acutis, as quoted in *Our Sunday Visitor*, October 11, 2023, "The Ultimate Collection of Blessed Carlo Acutis Quotes," www.oursundayvisitor.com.
21. Stein, *Philosophy of Psychology*, 235.
22. Stein, *Philosophy of Psychology*, 234–5.
23. T. S. Eliot, "The Waste Land," poetryfoundation.org.
24. Eliot, "The Hollow Men," allpoetry.com.
25. Eliot, "The Hollow Men," allpoetry.com.
26. Stein, *Philosophy of Psychology*, 235, italics given.
27. Stein, *Philosophy of Psychology*, 234–5.
28. Stein, *Life*, 277–8.
29. Stein, as quoted in Posselt, 60.
30. Stein, *Philosophy of Psychology*, 235.
31. Stein, *Science*, 10.
32. Stein, *Science*, 10.

33. Josef Pieper, *Only the Lover Sings: Art and Contemplation*, trans. Lothar Krauth (San Francisco: Ignatius Press, 1990) 35.
34. Stein, *Philosophy of Psychology*, 233–5.
35. Stein, *Philosophy of Psychology*, 85.
36. St. Thérèse of Lisieux, *Story of a Soul*, (Rockford, Illinois: Tan Books, 1997) 177.
37. Stein, *Philosophy of Psychology*, 85.
38. Stein, *Philosophy of Psychology*, 220.
39. Edith Stein, *On the Problem of Empathy*, trans. Waltraut Stein, Ph.D., 3rd rev. ed. *The Collected Works of Edith Stein*, Vol. 3, (Washington, DC: ICS Publications, 1989) 110–1.
40. Stein, *Empathy*, 11.
41. Stein, *Empathy*, 64.
42. Oben, *Life and Thought*, 48.
43. Gelber, in Introduction to *The Hidden Life*, xii, xiv.
44. Stein, *Woman*, 46.
45. Edith Stein, *Self-Portrait in Letters*, trans. Josephine Koeppel, OCD, ed. Dr. L. Gelber and Romaeus Leuven, OCD (Washington, DC: ICS Publications, 1993) Letter 38a, to Fritz Kaufmann.
46. Stein, *Woman*, 92.
47. Stein, *Woman*, 92, italics given.
48. Stein, *Woman*, 92–3.
49. Artistic Reference: Michelangelo Buonarroti, 1475–1564, *Madonna della Pietà*, 1498–1499, Papal Basilica of St. Peter in the Vatican, Vatican City.
50. Stein, *Finite*, 379.
51. Stein, *Finite*, 165, italics given.
52. Stein, *Empathy*, 10.
53. Stein, *Empathy*, 11.
54. Stein, *Empathy*, 32.
55. Stein, *Empathy*, 31.
56. Stein, *Empathy*, 32.
57. Nicholas Kardaras, *Glow Kids: How Screen Addiction is Hijacking our Kids—and How to Break the Addiction* (New York: St. Martin's Press, 2016) 8.
58. Charles Dickens, *A Christmas Carol* (Massachusetts: Candlewick Press, 2006) 34.

59. Dickens, *A Christmas Carol*, 32, 35.
60. Stein, *Science*, 12.
61. Stein, *Finite*, 379.
62. Stein, *Finite*, 379.
63. Stein, *Finite*, 379.
64. Stein, *Finite*, 379.
65. Stein, *Finite*, 379–80
66. Stein, *Finite*, 380, italics given.
67. Stein, *Finite*, 380, italics given.
68. Stein, *Finite*, 303.
69. Stein, *Finite*, 420.
70. Stein, *Finite*, 420.
71. Stein, *Science*, 12.
72. Stein, *Science*, 12.
73. Stein, *Science*, 12.
74. Stein, *Science*, 12. (Artistic Reference: St. John of the Cross, 1542–1591, *Christ of St. John of the Cross*, c. 1577, Monastery of the Incarnation, Avila).
75. Stein, *Self-Portrait in Letters*, Letter 328, to Mother Johanna van Weersth, OCD.
76. Stein, *Science*, 12–13.
77. Stein, *Science*, 13.
78. Edith Stein, *The Science of the Cross: A Study of St. John of the Cross*, trans. Hilda Graef, ed. Dr. L. Gelber and Romaeus Leuven, OCD, (London: Burns and Oates, 1960) 208, (pg. 275 in ICS Publications edition).
79. Edith Stein, *The Science of the Cross: A Study of St. John of the Cross*, trans. Josephine Koeppel, OCD, ed. Dr. L. Gelber and Romaeus Leuven, OCD, *The Collected Works of Edith Stein*, Vol. 6 (Washington, DC: ICS Publications, 2002) 9.
80. Stein, *Science*, 218–9, italics given.
81. St. John of the Cross, *Ascent of Mount Carmel*, 3. 35, as quoted in Stein, *Science*, 75–6.
82. Stein, *Philosophy of Psychology*, 161.
83. Pope St. John Paul II, *Letter of His Holiness Pope John Paul II to Artists* (Vatican City: Libreria Editrice Vaticana: 1999) n. 16.
84. Stein, *Philosophy of Psychology*, 213, 216.
85. Jad Hatem, "Il ritratto significante: la filosofia steiniana della creatività

artistica," Fall Lecture Series: Pontifical Gregorian University, Rome, 1999) italics given, translation mine.
86. Stein, *Philosophy of Psychology*, 213.
87. Stein, *Philosophy of Psychology*, 213.
88. Stein, *Life*, 396.
89. Stein, *Life*, 216–217.
90. Stein, *Life*, 339.
91. Giovanni della Croce, OCD, *Edith Stein: Santa Teresa Benedetta della Croce*, (Milano: Mimep-Docete, 1998) 117, translation mine.
92. Edith Stein, "How I Came to the Cologne Carmel," in *Selected Writings: With Comments and Reminiscences*, trans. and ed. Susanne Batzdorff (Springfield, Illinois: Templegate Publishers, 1990) 16.
93. Stein, *Self-Portrait in Letters*, Letter 112, to Elly Dursy (Sr. Mary Elizabeth of Divine Providence, OCD).
94. Stein, *Self-Portrait in Letters*, Letter 165, to Mother Petra Brüning, OSU.
95. Stein, *Self-Portrait in Letters*, Letter 178, to Mother Petra Brüning, OSU.
96. See Appendix, *Missa et Officium in Honorem B.V.M. Reginae Pacis*, EdithStein-Archiv, Karmel "Maria vom Frieden," Cologne, Germany, published in Elizabeth A. Mitchell, *Artist and Image: Artistic Creativity and Personal Formation in the Thought of Edith Stein* (Memphis: St. Paul Institute, 2021) https://stpaulmemphis.com/product/the-artist-the-image/.
97. Stein, *Philosophy of Psychology*, 220.
98. Stein, *Philosophy of Psychology*, 220.
99. Stein, *Philosophy of Psychology*, 220.
100. Stein, *Philosophy of Psychology*, 220.
101. Stein, *Philosophy of Psychology*, 130, italics given.
102. Stein, *Philosophy of Psychology*, 130, italics given.
103. Stein, *Philosophy of Psychology*, 130.
104. Stein, *Philosophy of Psychology*, 221–2.
105. Stein, *Philosophy of Psychology*, 279.
106. Stein, *Philosophy of Psychology*, 220–1.
107. Stein, *Philosophy of Psychology*, 279.
108. Stein, *Philosophy of Psychology*, 279.
109. *Lector, si monumentum requiris, circumspice.* Tomb of Sir Christopher Wren (1632-1723) St. Paul's Cathedral, London, UK, www.explore-stpauls.net.
110. Editor's note, *Philosophy of Psychology*, 131, note 10.

111. Stein, *Science*, 12.
112. Stein, *Woman*, 71.
113. Stein, *Finite*, 301.
114. Stein, *Finite*, 301, italics given.
115. Stein, *Finite*, 379.
116. Stein, *Finite*, 302.
117. Stein, *Finite*, 301.
118. Stein, *Finite*, 157–9, italics given.
119. Stein, *Finite*, 302, italics given.
120. Stein, *Finite*, 302.
121. Stein, *Finite*, 301–2.
122. St. John of the Cross, *Ascent of Mount Carmel*, 3. 35, as quoted in Stein, *Science*, 75–6.
123. Stein, *Finite*, 165.
124. Stein, *Finite*, 303–4, italics given.
125. Stein, *Finite*, 303–4, italics given.
126. Stein, *Finite*, 165.

4 THE ART OF SANCTITY

Often a person does not hear
The soft voice that speaks within ...
Then someone else must come,
Gifted with a finer ear attuned and keener sight,
And disclose the meaning of the obscure words.
This is the guide's wonderful gift.

Stein, from "I Am Always in Your Midst"[1]

But is art actually relevant? Could we not skip the artistic realm and move directly to contemplation of the divine in the abstract realm? Surely, the material artwork is secondary to the direct experience of beauty, truth, and goodness in God Himself? Stein, in fact, argues the opposite viewpoint. The artist is a vital guide, the artwork reveals the pure idea upon which it is based, and the encounter demands from us a lived response.

Becoming God's Masterpiece

The unfolding of our essence takes place as we become the person Our Lord created us to be. The essence of every human person encloses "all of the individual traits of (the individual's) character and all possible modes of his actions."[2] We spend our lives corresponding ever more fully to the perfect conception God has of us in His heart from all eternity. This process takes place in the quiet moments of prayer in which we seek His will, in the testing of daily life and perseverance in virtue, in the experiences of deep pain and loss which we surrender to Him. Our Lord has placed within us the individual traits which make us His unique creation. In His divine plan, He calls forth our gifts, our virtues, our personality, our temperament, our sense of humor, our gentle kindness, our undaunted courage, to fulfill His plan. "For the gifts and the calling of God are irrevocable," St. Paul affirms (Romans 11:29). And as St. John Henry Cardinal Newman exhorts in "The Mission of My Life" prayer: "God has created me to do Him some definite service. He has committed some work to me which He has not committed to another."

The person whom we become, Stein explains, blossoms from the deepest root of our essence. This essence unfolds as we live out our lives:

> The essence discloses itself when an *ability* passes over into the corresponding *doing*. The essence thus represents the deepest stratum in the entire structure: It is its "ground" ... which reaches from the deepest stratum to the surface, a root which grows into a tree and spreads out into the finest ramifications. And thus the vital activity is not "merely surface," but deeply rooted in the essence.[3]

Stein explains the maturation of the essence of St. John of the Cross into holiness of life with a similarly vivid description of the flourishing tree growing from a deep root:

> St. John's doctrine of the Cross could not be called a science of the Cross in our sense if it rested on a merely intellectual understanding. But it bears the genuine stamp of the Cross; it is the splendid top of a tree whose roots are in the depths of his soul, nourished by his heart's blood, and whose fruits are evident in his life.[4]

The unfolding of the individual essence of a poetic figure, in fact, follows the same pattern which occurs in the real unfolding of the actual human being. In this sense, the world of the poetic imagination is helpful for understanding the development of the human person. Stein turns to the Homeric epic the Iliad, and its protagonist Achilles, to highlight this concept:

> In the "world of Homer" things happen in precisely the same way as they do in the real world. Homer's characters

behave and are "construed" like real human beings: They have a nature or essence, and this nature or essence unfolds in their lives. And yet this entire Homeric world is not real: It is a "poetic world of appearances" and as such a product of *poetic imagination*.[5]

Our choices, our actions, and their consequences, contribute to the unfolding of our essence. The potential in the root of our person grows upward to the finest ramifications of the mature life we offer back to God, laden with realized gifts, completed actions, and fruitful holiness. Some aspects of our essence, however, may remain undeveloped, as Stein evidences through the character of Achilles:

> The loyalty of Achilles as a friend and his cruelty as an enemy, his gentleness and kindliness—these are obviously different traits of his character. But when he chases the fleeing Hector around the walls of Troy and later on even mutilates and desecrates the corpse of the slain enemy, there seems to be no trace left of any gentleness and kindliness. And when Achilles is seated with his mother by the shore of the sea pouring out his sorrow and allowing himself to be soothed by her consoling words, we might again not believe him capable of any inhuman cruelty. Thus we see how in his behavior now one and then the other essential trait of character prevails. What does not "express" itself in vital action remains hidden, not only veiled to our knowledge, but ontically undisclosed like the inner life of a closed bud.[6]

Achilles, the poetic character, has a level of existence which he does not realize in vital action. He has the potential to become a certain person, but these essential traits remain unrealized and unfulfilled in his actual life.

There is a poignant parallel here between the world of poetic imagination and our real lives. Aspects of our essence may remain unfulfilled by us, "like the inner life of a closed bud."[7] These traits are intended by Our Lord for a blossoming in our lives, but we fail to fulfill them in our living out of our call. When the Divine Artist is at work to bring forth these fruits in us, we can avoid His hand. We can rely on our limited understanding, instead of surrendering to His wisdom and His guidance. We may think we know best, and better than Our Lord, what needs to happen in our lives. We avoid the "gentle finger strokes" and the "chisel blows"[8] of the eternal Artist. As St. Paul says, "For I do not do the good I want, but the evil I do not want is what I do" (Romans 7:19).

To become all the Divine Artist intends, we must acquiesce to the guiding Hand of the Lord in obedience and trust. The Book of Proverbs encourages this correspondence with the will of God, exhorting, "Trust in the Lord with all your heart and rely not on your own understanding (Proverbs 3:5). Our Blessed Mother shows us the way to unite our will to His in loving surrender: "Behold the handmaid of the Lord; be it done to me according to Your word" (Luke 1:38). With such union of wills, Our Lady expresses her entire being, a perfect fulfillment of God's Love. Stein echoes this attitude of loving surrender, encouraging docility in the Lord's hands:

> What we can and must do is open ourselves to grace; that means to renounce our own will completely and to give it captive to the divine will, to lay our whole soul, ready for reception and formation, into God's hands.[9]

As a living artwork, then, we are a work in progress. With each moment on this earth, with every decision we make, word we speak, prayer we pray, act of love and trust, we allow God to call forth more fully the saint we have been created to become. To fulfill our divine purpose, we must strive to bring to fruition every essential trait He has placed within us. Often this flourishing of our true selves is a painful and arduous process. God Himself tells us, "Not for vengeance did the Lord put them in the crucible to try their hearts, nor has He done so with us. It is by way of admonition that He chastises those who are close to Him" (Judith 8:27).

We recall the many chisel blows and gentle finger strokes endured by Stein as she was formed into a saint by God. Her long night of searching for the Truth, her patient waiting to enter Carmel, being misunderstood by her family, giving up a brilliant academic career for the obscurity of Carmel, all refined her soul and perfected her character. In her journey to sanctity, even her temperament was refined from a forceful presence that could win any argument, to a gentle, serene, and reassuring disposition, in whom fluctuations of emotion became almost imperceptible. One audience member from a lecture in Münster observed, "My recollection of her is still fresh in my mind, for I was deeply impressed by her simplicity and modesty. She spoke slowly and calmly, without gesture but with great clarity and intensity."[10] Likewise, Stein's attitude in prayer revealed deep union with God, which edified others:

> Frequently I came across her in the chapel of the Marianum sunk deep in prayer. It was a moving experience to see her there, so completely absorbed in God that nothing could disturb or distract her. But when one went to have a word with her she was unassuming and always ready to help in an unobtrusive manner.[11]

Stein's personal bearing as a teacher formed her pupils even more directly than the subject matter she presented. One student from St. Magdalena's witnessed that "she was a still and silent person who led us only by what she *was*."[12] Yet another marveled, "You can't tell any longer what kind of temperament she has, because she has become perfectly balanced."[13]

As we allow Our Lord to mold and shape us, we become fully ourselves, as God intends. And He intends great good for us and through us. To bring the light of Christ to a darkened world, the Church needs saints, living, loving images of the Divine Life placed within us. He needed the fully refined and perfected Stein in Auschwitz. He needed her maternal heart, warm and clear, her ardent faith, and her sacrificial courage in the camps and cattle cars to which He led her.

Furthermore, as our lives authentically express that beauty which points to a deeper reality, to its mysterious source, our witness can transform the individuals with whom we come into contact. Our souls are the material in which this compelling Divine artwork is wrought:

> It is not inanimate material which must be entirely developed or formed in an exterior way, as is clay by the artist's hand or stone by the weather's elemental forces, it is rather a living formative root which possesses within itself the driving power (*inner form*) toward development in a particular direction; the seed must grow and ripen into the perfect gestalt, perfect creation."[14]

The growth and ripening of the seed into the perfect creation depends upon both interior and exterior factors. Our natural spiritual predisposition needs to be formed and properly developed. God Himself exists as "infinite plentitude and perfect or *pure* form because there is nothing in him that stands in need of formation, nor is there in him any possibility or potentiality of receiving extraneous influences."[15] God cannot become more fully God. He is perfect. Human beings, on the other hand, are not fully perfected. As finite creatures, we are imperfect and limited, and therefore we must be more perfectly developed:

> Though they are formed, they are not thoroughly formed, i.e., not formed to the extent of their ultimate perfection ... the creature can plastically mold itself by means of its own formative power, i.e., by means of the formative power of its own form, and the creature remains always open to the extraneous influences exerted by other creatures.[16]

The process of education therefore plays a vital role in assisting the complete development of each human person:

> We have seen that the soul can be developed only through activation of its faculties ... the senses, through impressions which they receive and process, the intellect through mental performance, the will through achievements which are characteristic to it, the emotions

through the variety of feelings, moods, and attitudes. Definite motives which place the faculties into motion are needed for all of this ... Thus we have attained a certain insight into the nature of education: the process of shaping the natural spiritual predisposition.[17]

Through education, effort, and with the help of grace, our natural spiritual predisposition is shaped. Our senses, our intellect, our will, and our emotions must be developed and refined through exertion and proper guidance. Stein turns again to the female literary characters of Sigrid Undset's Ingunn, Heinrich Ibsen's Nora, and Goethe's Iphigenie to exemplify how our soul is created for fulfillment. Maintaining that "it is through poetry that the soul is most adequately described,"[18] Stein presents the various levels of personal development exhibited by each character:

> Only if its faculties are correspondingly trained will the feminine soul be able to mature to that state conformable to its true nature. The concrete feminine types which we have cited represent to us not only diverse natural predispositions but also diverse formative levels of the soul of woman. We have seen in Ingunn a woman's soul which was nearly like unformed matter but which still permitted intuitions of its capacities. Another, Nora, through the influences of chance and social conventions, had found a certain formation but not that proper to her. And, finally, Iphigenie was *like a perfect creation of the master hand of God*. This presents us with the task of investigating what the formative powers are through which a woman's soul can be led to the nature for which it is intended and can be protected from the degeneration with which it is threatened.[19]

A "perfect creation of the master hand of God," such as we encounter in Iphigenie, is a soul who has fulfilled the purpose destined for her from all eternity. As Stein explains, "With Iphigenie, it is no longer a question of the breakthrough to true being; she *has* already achieved true being, in having reached the highest level of human perfection; she has only to put it to the test and allow it to have its effect. She longs that the level of being she has reached will serve as an instrument of that redeeming love which is her true destiny."[20] Leading the soul to the nature for which it is intended and protecting it from the degeneration with which it is threatened, then becomes the proper sphere and purpose of education.

In her own teaching profession, carried out for eight years as a Catholic professional before her entrance into the cloister of Carmel, Stein taught at the Dominican Teachers' Training Institute of St. Magdalena's in Speyer, Germany. In these years, Stein composed a series of *Aufsatzthemen* (*Essay Themes and Exam Topics*) for her students at St. Magdalena's. The manuscripts of Stein's *Essay Themes* were given to me by archivist Sr. M. Amata Neyer, OCD, curator of the Edith-Stein-Archiv in Cologne.[21] These precious documents, essentially Stein's own lesson plans, class assignments, and exam themes, show us exactly how Stein sought to form the spiritual capacity of her students. A few selections from the preparation for her "6th Class," including her assignment topics, reveal Stein's pedagogical approach:

> How can we structure our lessons so that the children can participate in them with joy?
> How is imagination taken into account in education?
> How does a visit to the theater affect the inner life of the young and what educational value does it have?
> How the teacher should be.[22]

For Stein, education is the essential formative process through which the person can properly mature and thus fulfill his destiny. As she notes, "The parable of the talents refers to the unique gift given to each individual; the Apostle's word describes the multiplicity of gifts afforded in the Mystical Body of Christ. The individual must discover his own unique gift."[23]

What, then, can best help us to discover our own unique gift? The finest attributes of the human spirit, exposure to beauty and truth, and encounter with the world beyond the veil, Stein maintains, are profoundly formative for the human person:

> Above all, these are human destinies and human actions as history and literature present them to the young—naturally this will be contemporary events as well. It is beauty in all its ramifications and the rest of the aesthetic categories. It is truth which prompts the searching human spirit into endless pursuit. It is everything which works in this world with the mysterious force and pull of another world.[24]

Stein showcases these human destinies and human actions in her *Essay Themes*. She presents as models to her students the characters and works which have been her intimate friends from her youth:

> What might Homer's poetic works have meant for the Greeks?
> How does Iphigenie fulfill her mission?
> Characteristics of "Brutus" in Shakespeare's Julius Caesar.
> Legend and Fairy Tale. (Comparison).
> On an Icelandic Farm.
> Anger ruins the best. (As shown in the argument between Agamemnon and Achilles).[25]

Through these and similar topics throughout her *Essay Themes*, Stein presents art, history, and literature "to guide the young person to perceive beauty and goodness."[26] Furthermore, the training of a person's ability to discriminate between the beautiful and the base is achieved through exposure to the best examples. "It is a matter," Stein explains, "of awakening joyful emotion for *authentic* beauty and goodness and disgust for that which is base and vulgar."[27] When we present young people with authentic examples of beauty and goodness, they learn to recognize the joyful effect of these influences. They begin to seek out the beautiful in imitation of what they have experienced. In my own classroom, I see Stein's wisdom in action daily. We enjoy the music of classical composers, playing quietly in the background of our study time throughout each day. Soon, the children identify the works of Handel, or Mozart, by ear, or they learn the refrain from an Aria such as Puccini's *Nessun dorma*, and they hum along to their favorite tunes. Slowly and almost imperceptibly, their souls are learning to experience joy in beauty. We also admire and discuss one great painting from Western Civilization each week. We might appreciate Peter Paul Rubens' *The Elevation of the Cross*, discussing the figures in the scene, the use of light and color, and the dramatic effect of the work. The children's aesthetic appreciation is refined, and they soon ask to be shown more examples of beautiful art and culture. Immersion in art and beauty offers an irreplaceable foundation in educational formation.

Finally, the role of the teacher, for Stein, is paramount. "Often the child is first awakened to the value of things by his awareness of the adult's responses—above all, that of the teacher—enthusiasm inspires enthusiasm."[28] Stein was known as a gifted and loving teacher herself. She would display a little sign in her dormitory window if her classes were to be conducted in the garden on a beautiful day. The Dominican sisters of Speyer even told me, on a personal visit to St. Magdalena's, how the students used to play loving pranks on Edith, hiding behind a garden wall to spray her with the hose, or surprising her on the pathway on the way to class. All of the give and take of the educational exchange involve the person of the teacher, and her personal example is essential. As Stein emphasizes, "it is of extraordinary significance that the child's education be placed in the hands of people who themselves have received proper emotional formation ... For women to be shaped in accordance with their authentic nature and destiny," Stein concludes, "they must be educated by authentic women."[29]

The formation of the child is particularly important because the child's openness to outside influences is simple and uninhibited. According to Stein, the child "receives and responds to impressions with unimpaired vigor and vitality, and with uninhibited simplicity ... The soul of the child is soft and impressionable. Whatever influence enters there can easily form it for a lifetime."[30] Stein calls this uninhibited simplicity of children, their inner openness, the "realism of the child."[31] By realism, Stein means the "original inner receptivity" of the soul.[32] She names children, saints, and artists, as uniquely characterized by this realism, or highly receptive interior disposition of the soul to respond authentically to experiences and impressions. The uninhibited simplicity of the child surely underlies the Lord's exhortation to "suffer the little children to come unto me and forbid them not; for of such is the kingdom of Heaven" (Matthew 19:14). The child does not put up a wall of pretense or the buffer of rationalization when encountering the world. The child assumes, for instance, that everyone he meets is a friend. He puts up no defenses or calculation towards the stranger. This openness of the child, furthermore, demands careful formative attention.

In a lecture entitled "The Church, Woman, and Youth," given at Augsburg in 1931, Stein addresses our responsibility to form the child properly, observing that "the child's soul receives impressions from what he sees, hears, and touches; indeed, even experiences before birth can leave impressions upon the soul, and these impressions can have unpredictable consequences in later life. Therefore," she notes, "the mother must keep pure the atmosphere in which the child is living."[33] The world of faith can also be presented to the child with positive results, since "the pure uncorrupted child's heart has no difficulties in this and asks for more and more." [34] The child's soul is open to the fullness of the faith, and their receptive souls respond readily to models of holiness, the lives of the saints, the stories of Scripture, and the mysteries of the Faith.

Stein herself exhibited a highly perceptive and sensitive temperament from her earliest years. She had a deep interior existence and was a finely tuned, pensive child. "Within me," Stein reveals, "… there was a hidden world. Whatever I saw or heard throughout my days was pondered over there."[35] She relates the extent to which her earliest experiences penetrated her sensitive soul:

> The sight of a drunkard could haunt and plague me for days and nights on end ... Should anyone speak of a murder in my presence, I would lie awake for hours that night, and, in the dark, horror would press in upon me from every corner. Indeed, even a somewhat coarse expression which, in irritation, my mother once used in my presence, pained me so deeply that I could never forget this minor incident, an argument with my eldest brother.[36]

Stein's choice of the verbs *verfolgen*, *quälen*, and *kriechen* to describe the sight of the drunkard literally "pursuing" and "torturing" her day and night, as well as a horror which "crept" toward her in the darkness, vividly reveals the depth of inner impressionability of her child's soul.

Stein also describes her sensitive reaction to a dramatic work, which affected her during childhood. The drama of Friedrich Schiller's *Mary Stuart* captured the imagination of the young Stein. She had not yet read it, but had only heard it referenced, in fact, when her perceptive soul reacted to the drama:

> My family often recounted one such instance. When I was about five years old, my sister Frieda was reading *Mary Stuart* in school and was then allowed to go to see the stage play with my mother. Before they went, there was a great deal of talk about it; and, as usual, I picked up far more than was intended for me. While the two were at the theater, my feverish fantasies began and I cried out, over and over, in great excitement, "Oh, *do* cut off Elizabeth's head!"
>
> I recall what a sequel there was to this incident. The following year, when I went to school and had arrived at barely managing to read words in print, I searched out the proper volume of Schiller's works in our bookcase at home, took it to the kitchen and asked my mother whether I might read to her out of *Mary Stuart*.
>
> Very solemnly she said: "Go ahead, read."
>
> How far I got at that time, I cannot remember. But it is easy to surmise that such sudden outbursts alarmed my

relatives. They called it "nerves" and tried, as much as possible, to shield me from overexcitement.[37]

Stein's interest in this literary drama, in fact, continues into her adult teaching years, and she makes specific references to the drama in the *Essay Themes* which she wrote for her teacher preparation courses.

Although aware of her own sensitive nature, the young Stein did not often express such perceptions outwardly, a situation which increased her inner turmoil:

> I never mentioned a word to anyone of these things which caused me so much hidden suffering. It never occurred to me that one could speak about such matters. Only infrequently did I give my family any inkling of what was happening: for no apparent reason I sometimes developed a fever and in delirium spoke of the things which were oppressing me inwardly.[38]

As she reached the age of reason, a "great transformation"[39] took place within Stein. "Gradually my inner world grew lighter and clearer. Whatever was heard, seen, read, or experienced offered my active fantasy material for the most intrepid constructions."[40] Stein comes to understand the importance of expressing her perceptions outwardly. "What one cannot express," she notes, "remains dark and gloomy in the soul, and whoever is unable to express himself is imprisoned in his own soul; he is unable to liberate himself and cannot relate to others."[41]

Stein's ability to express herself in literary form, through poems and dramatic dialogues, is a mark of the artist, while her ultimate expression of faith and love in laying down her life in martyrdom is the mark of the saint. She has noted that children, saints, and artists exhibit a realism which responds to experiences with deep, genuine authenticity, in contrast to the degeneration of human nature which suffers from an "inability to perceive and respond to facts interiorly in a way that corresponds to their authentic value."[42]

Like the openness of children, Stein explains, saints possess a "holy realism" which allows them to experience reality with the "original inner receptivity of the soul reborn by the Holy Spirit."[43] Whatever the soul of the saint encounters "is received in an appropriate manner and with corresponding depth, and finds in the soul a living, mobile, docile energy that allows itself to be easily and joyfully led and molded by that which it has received, unhampered by any mistaken inhibitions and rigidity."[44] What the saint experiences infuses their receptive soul. The saint responds authentically to the call of faith with inner joy and openness.

Stein is aware that there are those who "are depressed because the facts of salvation history do not at all (or no longer) impress them as they ought."[45] Perhaps they have heard the Gospel and have disregarded the message. They hear the call to conversion and respond with indifference. The soul which responds with *holy realism*, in contrast, "demonstrates to them how things should actually be: where there is genuine, lively faith, there the doctrine of faith and the 'tremendous deeds' of God are the content of life. All else steps aside for it and is determined by it."[46]

The entire reality of the saint is determined by the reality of God. Mother Teresa of Calcutta hears the words "as long as you did it to one of the least of these" (Matthew 25:40), and she commits her life to the poorest of the poor in the slums and the alleyways of Calcutta. St. Maximilian Kolbe hears the words "greater love has no man than this" (John 15:13), and he lays down his life for a condemned prisoner in Auschwitz. This response of lived, genuine faith is the holy realism of the saints in action. "Such realism, when it leads a holy soul to accept the truths of faith, becomes *the science of the saints*,"[47] Stein proclaims. The science of the saints animates Stein's self-offering in martyrdom in Auschwitz. In this act of union with Christ's sacrifice on the Cross, the fulfillment of Stein's essence is complete. The mystery of the cross becomes the inner form of her life, and her life is transformed into a science of the cross.

Artist and Image

The union of childlike realism and holy realism, combined with artistic realism in one individual, furthermore, has the capacity to profoundly transform the artwork created. A look at St. John of the Cross as an artist confirms Stein's analysis. In her extensive study of St. John of the Cross's artistic and holy realism in *The Science of the Cross*, Stein emphasizes that St. John was not only a deeply holy mystic, but a genuine artist:

> In John's case, a third factor must be taken into consideration: he had an artistic nature. Among the various crafts and arts in which the boy tested himself were those of carver and painter. We still have drawings he made later in his life. (His sketch of the Ascent of Mount Carmel is generally known.) When he was prior in Granada he drew up the blueprints for a contemplative monastery. He was a poet as well as a visual artist. He had a need to express in songs that which transpired in his soul. His mystical writings are merely additional explanations of all he expressed directly in his poetry. And so, in his case, we must reckon also with the characteristic realism of an artist.[48]

St. John's spiritual poetry flows from his deep interior experience. In fact, as Stein notes, "childlike, artistic, and holy realism were combined in him and supplied for the message of the cross the most favorable soil in which it could grow into the science of the cross."[49] The artist, Stein affirms, "is akin to the child and the saint … in the confident strength of his impressionability."[50] For Stein, the artistic temperament is marked by "a higher susceptibility, a greater aliveness than that allotted to others."[51] What distinguishes this impressionability of the artist, furthermore, is that the artist is compelled to form an image, to create an artwork, in response to their deep experience. Artistic realism is distinguished from childlike and holy realism by the artist's creation of this artwork in response to interior experience. "It is characteristic of the artist to transform into image anything that causes an interior stirring and demands to be expressed exteriorly."[52]

Stein further clarifies that "image here is not to be restricted to the visual arts; it must be understood to refer to any artistic expression including the poetic and musical."[53] The artist experiences a glorious sunset and must capture it on the canvas. The artist suffers loss or grief and composes a musical score to express the emotion. Stein, the artist, confronts two philosophical schools and creates a dialogue between the characters of Edmund Husserl and St. Thomas Aquinas to dramatize the discussion. She hears Our Lord's call to self-offering and beckons the character of Queen Esther to illuminate her dramatic poetry in prophetic response.

We see St. John's expressive gift, moreover, in the images of the Cross and Night which appear frequently throughout his poetic works. Stein points out, however, that the image of the Cross draws upon an established meaning, while John's Night-symbolism has been fashioned poetically. She attributes St. John's identity as an artist, therefore, to this formation of Night-symbolism in his poems. She emphasizes that "the prevailing symbol in (John's) poems, as in his treatises, is not the cross, but night ... That the night-symbol prevails is a sign that the poet and mystic is spokesman in the writings of the Holy Doctor of the Church rather than the theologian."[54] In other words, a creative fashioning was employed by St. John in the crafting of Night symbolism. The *holy realism* of St. John experienced spiritual night, and the *artistic realism* of St. John fashioned the poetic image of night in response.

Stein further delineates the artistic contrast between the function of both Cross and Night in St. John's poetry, in which the Cross is expressed through an established sign-relation, while Night is expressed through a creative image-fashioning. The Cross, Stein explains, "is not merely a *natural object* but rather a *tool* finished and used by human hands for a very specific purpose. As a tool, it has played an incomparably important role in history. Everyone who lives in a Christian cultural sphere knows something about this role."[55] The concept of suffering which St. John evokes in his use of the Cross, therefore, calls upon an historically established meaning:

> The cross in its visible form leads immediately to the fullness of meaning which is entwined with it. It is thus a sign, but one that has not artificially gained meaning; rather it has genuinely earned it by reason of its effectiveness and its history. Its visible form indicates the meaning connected with it. Therefore we can rightly call it an *emblem*.[56]

The Cross and its meaning are connected objectively, and no poetic interpretation is needed for our understanding of the sign. In contrast to this established relationship employed when speaking of the Cross, John's Night-symbolism is the result of the creative fashioning of his artistic sensibility. St. John's artistic and holy soul was highly receptive to the beauty of both the natural and spiritual realities of night. "We know from testimonies about his life and from his poems, that he was extremely sensitive to the cosmic night with all its tonalities. He spent entire nights gazing over the wide landscape from a window or out into the open."[57] St. John's understanding of mystical night, moreover, is the fruit of his profound spiritual receptivity to a night which "is not to be understood in a cosmic sense. It does not impose itself on us from without but rather has its origin in the interior of the soul."[58] Through his artistic realism, St. John leads us through the symbol of his night-image to the fullness of meaning of spiritual night which he has experienced in his holy realism.

The mystical and the natural beauties of night have touched John's holy and artistic sensitivities. His artistic realism fashions a connection between the two. He transfers the attributes of the cosmic to the mystical experience. The connection which he crafts between natural night and spiritual night is permitted through a similarity in the content of both nights. His interior experience of the full meaning of night emerges through the symbolic image he creates. In so doing, John "found words to describe night which no other bard of the night has surpassed."⁵⁹ Stein presents Stanza 15 of John's *Spiritual Canticle* as evidence:⁶⁰

La noche sosegada	The tranquil night, the lovely one,
En par de los levantes de la aurora	Already pierced by new morn's light,
La música callada,	Music of the softest tones
La soledad sonora,	And solitude that rings,
La cena, que recrea,	The supper that refreshes and
y enamora.	Lends love wings.

Through his poetic imagery John connects cosmic and mystic night. In doing so he moves beyond the basic image-relation involving "two known things that could come into this relation for the sake of a certain objective commonness."⁶¹ Instead, he presents us with a profoundly understood "relationship of *symbolic expression*" in which "something unknown and inaccessible" is evoked "through something commonly known and familiar."⁶² The unknown and inaccessible experience of John's spiritual night is evoked for us through the commonly known and familiar features of cosmic night. Through John's artwork we encounter a fullness of spiritual meaning uniquely experienced by the artist and saint and made available to us through his image. We are brought into connection with a hitherto unknown meaning by his art.

The ability of image-language to veil or reveal its meaning, Stein notes, was appreciated by Christ Himself. The Lord often favored the use of parables and imagery in communicating the things of God. "How else," Stein questions, "would it be possible for so many to 'have eyes yet see not, have ears yet hear not'? How could the same language that reveals divine truth be at the same time a veil concealing it from another?"⁶³ The image can both reveal meaning and yet leave some meaning veiled. The entire communication takes place through a mysterious correspondence of meanings between the tangible and the intangible:

> There exists an original mutuality and an objective correspondence that enables the sensory to reveal knowl-

edge of the spiritual ... Something intangible here and something intangible there and yet clearly one overlays the other and can be used to access the other, not by arbitrary choice and systematic comparison but in *symbolic experience* that strikes upon *primitive connections* and thus finds a necessary figuration for what is conceptually unutterable.[64]

Karol Wojtyla, later to become Pope St. John Paul II, likewise observes in his doctoral study, *Faith According to Saint John of the Cross*, that the writings of St. John "are not simply speculative treatises on mystical theology; they are a witness to a mystical experience."[65] Like Stein, Wojtyla asserts St. John's demonstration of how these truths "can be expressed much more vividly after one has actually experienced them."[66] Alluding to this transformative effect of mystical experience upon St. John's artistic expression, Stein observes:

> We already hear the cry of longing with which the *Song* begins: *A donde te escondiste?* (Where have you hidden yourself?), the plaint of a soul wounded in the depth of her heart by the love of God. She knows her Lord, and surely not only "from hearsay," but has personally met him, has experienced his touch in her inmost region.[67]

John, the artist and saint, wrote his *Canticle*, furthermore, while imprisoned in the dungeon of Toledo. The artistic heart of St. John sings more intensely of the beauty from which he is separated and longs to experience once again. "This *Song* from the prison is of overwhelming richness in images and thoughts. In this way it is essentially different from the stanzas of the *Dark Night* and *The Living Flame of Love*."[68] The more intense imagery stems directly from the heightened experience of the imprisoned artist's soul:

> Here the soul and the whole of creation are in movement. This is not simply a difference in the literary style: the difference in style arose out of a deep-seated difference of the experience behind the writing ... The *Spiritual Canticle* ... is written by a soul that is most intensely

> gripped by the visible charms of creation. With wonderful images and enchanting sounds, the world outside, the world from which he is cut off, invades the cell of the prisoner, who is a poet and sculptor, one susceptible to the magic of music.[69]

St. John's poetry is enflamed with the mystery of the ineffable. This saint "does not pause at the picture and sounds. They are for him mysterious hieroglyphics that express—and in which he himself is able to express—what transpires concealed in a soul. The hieroglyphics are truly *mysterious*. They contain such a fullness of meaning that it seems impossible to the saint himself to find the right words in order to explain all that the Holy Spirit sang within him 'in inexpressible groanings.'"[70] He offers a glimmer of the "unknown and inaccessible" Supreme Beauty through the "known and familiar" attributes of his created image.[71] We arrive through this symbolic relation, then, at the infinite fullness of meaning which has impressed itself upon St. John's holy and perceptive soul.

The artwork which the artist fashions through his gift of artistic realism has therefore what Stein calls a revelatory power. All genuine art is revelation, for Stein, because every genuine artwork is a symbol, or meaning-picture. "Every genuine work of art is ... a *symbol* (Sinnbild) ... that is, it comes from that infinite fullness of *meaning* into which every bit of human knowledge is projected to grasp something positive and speak of it. It does so in such a manner, in fact, that it mysteriously suggests the whole fullness of meaning, which for all human knowledge is inexhaustible."[72]

Stein presents a further analysis of the artwork as symbol in an essay submitted for publication in 1941 but never published in her lifetime. On May 9, 1940, Sr. Teresa Benedicta a Cruce had received a letter in the Echt Carmel informing her that she had been made a charter member of the International Phenomenological Society, recently established in the United States by philosophy professor Marvin Farber and Stein's friend of university years Fritz Kaufmann. Farber's communication invited Stein to "consider sending us an essay for the journal that is based upon any work that you have done in the past." Stein submitted the study entitled "Ways to Know God: The 'Symbolic Theology' of Dionysius the Areopagite and Its Objective Presuppositions" to the society's periodical *Philosophy and Phenomenological Research*, on September 12, 1941, noting, "I believe you have made your parameters wide enough to include something like this. My superiors do leave me full liberty; but it is, of course, self-evident that I cannot write on anything that has nothing at all to do with our life."[73] Stein would be dead at the hands of the Nazis less than one year after submitting the article.

Stein's investigation was drafted as a preliminary contribution to a larger work she was compiling on Dionysius the Areopagite. The article was never published during her lifetime, as disagreement ensued over the article's suitability for publication by the International Phenomenological Society, and delays occurred in finding either a translator or another journal for its English publication. Ironically, the article intended by Stein for publication in an American journal first appeared in Louvain, Belgium, in Stein's original German, at the arrangement of Dr. Lucy Gelber in 1946, a few months before its American publication in the July 1946 edition of *The Thomist*, in a translation by Rudolf Allers of the Catholic University of America.

In her penetrating analysis, Stein asserts that "we can only note how indispensable symbolic knowledge is for any aesthetic view of the world as well as for the creation, understanding, and enjoyment of works of art."[74] For Stein, the artwork speaks to us, offers us a glimpse, of that fullness of meaning from which it comes and to which it directs our gaze. The musical notes or the words of the poem point us to the fuller reality which they express. The expression of a line of music, just as the expression of a human face, provides access to the fullness of meaning which it reveals. "Without 'expression,'" Stein insists, "we would have no access to the being of someone else's soul."[75] Expression provides the window to the deeper reality. "Everything bodily is either a 'mirror' or an expression of something of the soul."[76] We come to understand another's experience when this experience is revealed through outward expression such as a look in the eye, a smile on the face, or a subtle depth of gaze. "A single action and also a single bodily expression, such as a look or a laugh," Stein describes, "can give me a glimpse into the kernel of the person."[77]

We glimpse the kernel of the person, and we comprehend something of their deeper reality, the mystery of their individual personhood. The precious photographs which we have of Stein span from her childhood, through her academic years, to her religious life and her final image, taken for a passport photo, in which she gazes upwards, her eyes alight. We encounter a glimpse of her person through these serious and serene snapshots. We grasp something of her inner depth through her outward expression.

Just as the individual is glimpsed through outward manifestation, so too, God Himself reveals His divinely mysterious Being through His exterior expression. All the aspects of the natural world point to their Creator, in fact, Who can be recognized through them:

> God portrayed Himself, in the object He formed and through it lets Himself be known. That He is not already known beforehand and hence is not recognized, "known again," does not invalidate the notion of the image as copy, likeness, made *from* something. After all, in a good portrait we can not only recognize a person we know but also meet a stranger. And by looking at a good portrait we can tell that it is a *portrait* and that it is a *good* one. This is surely an objective possibility even if not everyone can do it, but only somebody with a "flair" for it, a trained eye. And what we mean by "symbol" today, it seems to me, is most properly fulfilled precisely when we take a graphic form as a symbol or "meaning-picture" and the image discloses to us for the first time a meaning that was hitherto unknown to us.[78]

When the artwork is genuine, when it faithfully portrays the idea upon which it is based, the artwork reveals a meaning that was hitherto unknown. There is, furthermore, an interplay between forming and imitating which takes place in the creation of the image by the artist. Stein delineates the three determining aspects of the image: it is fashioned or shaped, it can be clearly grasped, and the image points to its content "as a *figure* points to its fulfillment or as a *copy* or *likeness* points to its *original* or *type*."[79] The image is in some way tangible, it can be perceived by the senses. It has a commonality with the idea it represents, to which it points as its meaning and origin. It is "something graphic, intuitive, such as may be met with in sense perception," which "represents something else in virtue of an objective commonness enabling us to recognize the one in the other."[80] We encounter the idea through the image, the imperceptible archetype through its perceivable manifestation.

The more closely the created work adheres to the archetype upon which it based, furthermore, the more fully the work is a masterpiece in the realm of craftsmanship. Michelangelo's *Pietà* is considered an artistic masterpiece because the sculpture so closely resembles in marble expression the archetype of the artwork in the artist's mind. Likewise, the Divine Archetype is made present in His creation, and we see Him, hear Him, experience Him, through His re-created likeness in image. The near perfect resemblance of the artwork to its archetype is the signature of the Master Craftsman.

God Himself is characterized as an artist precisely by His creation in image. He expresses Himself in image form and in the Word. The entire universe is a boundless expression of His creative love. He is the Divine Artist expressing Himself eternally in His works. His creative gift is an endless wellspring, so profound that we are often unable to grasp the fullness of His expression. American playwright Thornton Wilder, in fact, declares that it is the saints and artists who have a unique ability to perceive God's creative gift more fully than others. In the piercing Final Act of his play *Our Town*, Wilder confronts us with the questioning of Emily Webb, a young woman who has died and has returned to visit daily life from the perspective of eternity. Emily has watched the people she once knew going through their daily routine, blind to the precious, irreplaceable, unfathomable gift of life. She realizes what human beings so often do not understand. She comprehends the depth of grace in the ordinary gifts of everyday life, and she poignantly asks:

> Do any human beings ever realize life while they live it?—every, every minute?

To which the all-knowing Stage Manager replies:

> No. *Pause.* The saints and poets, maybe—they do some.[81]

Only from the perspective of eternity will we be able to fully grasp the magnificence of the work of the Divine Artist, in ourselves and in the entire world permeated with His creative gifts.

The Divine Artist

God is the Divine Artist. He portrays Himself in the objects He forms, and through them lets Himself be known. As we come to know a person through their portrait, so we come to know God through the meaning-pictures by which He reveals Himself. We, in our turn, imitate the image forming nature of God.

The defining characteristic of the artist is his formation of the image. This image formation, which is fundamental to artistic creativity, finds its foundation in the image-forming nature of the Divine Godhead. Stein addresses this relationship in her discussion of "The Contrast Between the Creator and His Creation and the Image Relationship" in *Finite and Eternal Being*:

> Because God is spirit, he is fully transparent to himself and generates from eternity the "image" that pertains to his own being, an image in which he sees himself as he is in himself—his co-essential Son, Eternal Wisdom, or the Word ... (who) is the universal archetype of the deter-

minateness of all creaturely essences or natures, the eternal paradigm of everything they are destined to be.[82]

The Holy Spirit, Stein goes on to observe, "is the archetype of all creaturely life and efficacious action as well as of that spiritual radiance of their essence or nature which is a property even of material structures."[83] This radiance of the Holy Spirit always points to and reveals God the Father, who "as the primary unconditional principle" is seen in "every independent actuality (*ousia*)."[84] When the human spirit forms creatively out of proportionate matter, therefore, this action is in imitation of the divine spirit, Who generates from eternity in image:

> That which is not pure spirit is a structure that is formed by spirit, either immediately by the divine spirit or mediately by created forms out of proportionate matter ... In their unity of meaning and life, all created structures are images of the divine essence from which they are distinguished by their materiality ... We thus look, in the Triune Deity for the archetype of what in the realm of creaturely being we have designated as meaning and fullness of life.[85]

To explain how our perception of the divine archetype through the image occurs, Stein turns to an analysis of beauty and the uniquely human spiritual capacity to experience joy in beauty, in her final philosophical work *Finite and Eternal Being*. Stein's work presents, in what she calls "a book written by a beginner for beginners,"[86] a synthesis of Thomistic and phenomenological thought through an exploration of the meaning of being. With her entrance into the Catholic faith, Stein encountered the rich intellectual tradition of the greatest Catholic minds. Her own academic work in turn sought to amalgamate her philosophical foundations with her newfound intellectual patrimony:

> At an age when others may confidently call themselves teachers, the author was compelled to start all over again ... She had found the way to Christ and his church ... She naturally felt an increased desire to familiarize herself

> with the intellectual foundations of this world ... St. Thomas found a reverent and willing pupil. Her mind, however, was no longer a *tabula rasa*: It had already received the firm impress of her philosophical training, which could not be ignored. Her reason had become the meeting place of two philosophic worlds which demanded a dialectic elucidation.[87]

Within this intellectual conversation between phenomenology and the world of St. Thomas, Stein addresses the nature of beauty. For Stein, beauty "denotes that quality in an existent by virtue of which this existent is capable of causing satisfaction."[88] This satisfaction is an "act of the spirit," since "even sensuous beauty can (*as* beauty) be only intellectually conceived."[89] This is a connection to which St. Thomas Aquinas points, Stein explains, "when he emphasizes that it is especially the higher ('spiritual') senses which are instrumental in making possible our access to the beautiful ... and that *only a human being* but not an irrational animal, *finds joy in beauty*."[90]

What, then, is this spiritual power which is "ordained to the beautiful and finds its perfection in satisfaction?"[91] For her answer, Stein turns to Aristotle's definition of the beautiful as "characterized by order, harmony, and due determinateness."[92] She asserts that the spirit "is itself determined in its measure and species and proceeds in its activity in accordance with its own intrinsic order."[93] In responding to beauty, the spirit recognizes something which pertains to its own being. The sensation of joy in response to the beautiful, therefore "must be that same peculiar *sense* of the spirit for *measure, due determinateness*, and *order* in which Aristotle discerned the foundation of beauty."[94]

Stein points out that a similar view has been expressed by St. Thomas, who observes that "'we call beautiful that which pleases when it is seen (*quae visa placent*). Beauty, therefore, is constituted by due proportion. For the senses find joy in things which are duly ordered or proportioned (*in rebus debite proportionatis*), in things which are, as it were, proportioned in a certain similitude with the senses.'"[95] It is intrinsic to the spiritual capacity of man, Stein concludes, to perceive right order and to respond to it with satisfaction:

> The created spirit (particularly in its knowledge) as an existent is not only in accord with all other existents in that it, too, is permeated by the law and order of all that which is, but as spirit is distinguished by the prerogative of becoming aware experientially of this accord. And this experiential awareness we designate as "satisfaction," as "enjoyment of beauty," or "aesthetic joy."[96]

The human soul is uniquely distinguished by the ability to experience joy in beauty. What, then, is the fundamental source of beauty itself? The answer is of divine origin:

> If beauty is a property of the existent as such (and thus a genuinely transcendental determination) it cannot pertain exclusively to created existents … Just as there is divine truth and divine goodness which are the ultimate ground or cause of everything that is true and good, so there must also be divine beauty as the ultimate ground or cause of everything that is beautiful.[97]

All beauty manifested in created existents finds its source in "supreme beauty—beauty as such."[98] The existence of the Divine Being behind the value of beauty which we perceive explains our soul's response. In encountering beauty, we are, in fact, responding to an encounter with God Himself, manifested to us through His attribute of beauty:

> God is perfect being without any want, fault, or flaw. Even if for us he remains undefinable and immeasurable—because his infinity transcends all human measures and determinations—he is nevertheless his own measure, determined in himself in "duly proportioned" accord with himself, and wholly luminous in and for himself: that eternal light "in whom there is no shadow of darkness."[99]

Of St. Thomas's definition of the three essential characteristics of beauty: "'1) *integrity* or perfection (for what is deformed or defective is for this very reason ugly); 2) *due proportion* or harmony; and 3) *clarity*,'"[100] it is through clarity, Stein asserts, that beauty acts upon the soul in an unmistakable way:

> The "clarity" is like a splendor of brightness poured out over the existent, revealing the latter's divine origin. And it seems that this word "clarity" gives voice to the true enchantment of the beautiful. It expresses what the average human being means by "beauty" and what has such a mysterious hold on the human soul. Just as in knowing we gain an "authentic understanding" of the nature of truth and in the fulfillment of our striving an authentic understanding of the nature of goodness, so we begin to understand the nature of beauty when that "splendor" touches our soul."[101]

When the splendor of beauty touches our soul, we respond with joy. This splendor is encountered "in the world of sense in the radiance of physical light, without which all sensuous beauty would remain hidden from us. We meet it in the radiance of color and in the loveliness of physical forms and bodies."[102]

But, is this splendor limited to realities in the tactile world and physical objects? No, this revelation of the existent's divine origin, Stein argues, "is by no means confined to the world of sense."[103] What further beauty is included in this encounter with the divine? "There is spiritual beauty," Stein reminds us. "There is the *beauty of the human soul*, whose 'ways and actions are duly measured and ordered in accordance with the intellectual clarity of reason.'"[104]

We have all experienced an encounter with the beauty of the human soul. For Stein, the splendor of the human soul touched by grace surpasses all natural manifestations of beauty. "Inasmuch as every created thing is an image of a divine *Urbild* (archetype), due measure coincides with essential truth."[105] In the artistic realm, an existent is more perfect the greater its congruity with its archetype, and perfection is correlated to the beautiful.

So too in the spiritual realm, the perfect union of our souls with the divine will manifests the splendor of the Divine Being. The clarity or radiance which enchants us in an artistic work, is even more fully manifested through the living being who achieves a most perfect correspondence with the divine archetype through *sanctity*. The Divine Being shines forth most powerfully through the human person most perfectly united to His will.

Our souls are created in the image and likeness of God. When our souls respond in perfect correspondence to the Divine Creator's intention for our lives, the revelation of His divine splendor pours forth from us. The moving power of divine beauty finds its ultimate expression in the life of the soul in union with God:

> The closer a created being is to the divine *Urbild*, the more perfect it is. This is why intellectual and spiritual beauty range above sensuous beauty ... Because the human soul by divine grace is drawn near to the divine being in an entirely new sense, the splendor which grace pours out over a human soul surpasses all purely natural brightness and harmony."[106]

Ultimately, the beauty of the divine *Urbild* is most perfectly revealed through the person of Jesus Christ, in whom the divine archetype manifested through union with the divine will is perfectly expressed. "In the course of (St. Thomas's) discussion of the distinctions among the Divine Persons he attributes beauty in a preeminent degree to the Son."[107] The correlation of perfection and beauty provides the basis for this reality:

> An existent is perfect when it is wholly what it ought to be, when nothing is wanting to it, and when it has attained to the highest measure of its being. This perfection denotes the congruity of the existent with the divine idea which is its archetype, (essential truth), and simultaneously with the divine will (essential goodness). Whatever is perfect is true, good, and beautiful.[108]

We turn to Our Lady and the Saints as such masterpieces of the Divine Artist, souls who most perfectly represent in lived experience the Divine intention for their lives. Stein lovingly describes Our Lady's radiant beauty:

> In the statement "I am the handmaid of the Lord," Mary's whole being is articulated. It bespeaks her readiness to serve the Lord and excludes every other relationship ... She is the mother of the living not because all succeeding generations come from her but because her maternal love embraces the whole Mystical Body with Jesus Christ its head ... Thus we can see the prototype of the feminine being in the Spirit of God poured out over creatures. It finds its *most perfect image* in the purest Virgin who is the bride of God and mother of all mankind.[109]

In her own surrender to the divine will and her union of spirit with Our Lord's intention for her life, St. Edith Stein, furthermore, radiates as a masterpiece of God. Her spirituality is permeated with surrender to the Lord's guidance, an openness to Him which she terms "living at the Lord's hand."[110] She follows His plans for her with loving surrender:

> What did not lie in *my* plan lay in *God's* plans. And the more often such things happen to me the more lively becomes in me the conviction of my faith that—from God's point of view—nothing is *accidental*, that my entire life, even in the most minute details, was pre-designed in the plans of divine providence.[111]

This union with the Lord's will, Stein explains, cannot be achieved through sheer force of effort but must be "effected by grace."[112] Through grace the woman's soul can become "expansive, quiet, empty of self, warm and clear," as "a single total condition of the soul."[113] Stein was known for this serene interior recollection and profound inner warmth. Even in the chaos, filth, and upheaval of the Westerbork Camp after her arrest, Stein is described by fellow prisoner Julius Markan as sublimely recollected and loving. Markan relates:

> Among the prisoners who were brought in on 5 August, Sr. Benedicta stood out on account of her great calmness

and composure. The distress in the barracks, and the stir caused by the new arrivals, was indescribable. Sr. Benedicta was just like an angel, going around among the women, comforting them, helping them and calming them. Many of the mothers were near to distraction; they had not bothered about their children the whole day long, but just sat brooding in dumb despair. Sr. Benedicta took care of the little children, washed them and combed them, looked after their feeding and their other needs. During the whole of her stay there, she was so busy washing and cleaning as acts of lovingkindness that everyone was astonished.[114]

Such lovingkindness in calm solicitude towards others is precisely what Stein understood to be the fruit of a true contemplative vocation. As she affirms in a letter to a Dominican religious during her time at St. Magdalena's in Speyer, "even in the contemplative life, one may not sever the connection with the world. I even believe," she continues, "that the deeper one is drawn into God, the more one must 'go out of oneself'; that is, one must go to the world in order to carry the divine life into it."[115] Stein's understanding of the "divine life" pours from her in a symphony of vocational love:

> The motive, principle and goal of the religious life is to surrender to God entirely in self-forgetting love, allowing one's own life to end in order to make room in oneself for God's life.
>
> The more completely this is realized the more is the soul filled with the riches of divine life. But divine life is love, overflowing, undemanding love freely giving itself; love that in compassion bends down to every creature in need; love that heals the sick and awakens the dead to life; love that protects and shelters, nourishes, teaches and shapes us; love that mourns with the mourners, rejoices with the joyful, and puts itself at the service of every creature so that each creature may become what the Father wishes it to be—in a word: the love of the Divine Heart.[116]

St. Edith Stein ultimately becomes the love of the Divine Heart, overflowing and freely giving itself, through her witness of martyrdom. Her final act of loving response to the divine reality, in imitation of Christ's sacrificing and selfless love, radiates with the splendor of a masterpiece in the realm of faith. This divine splendor pours forth from the life of St. Edith Stein as a beacon of hope against overwhelming despair and of courage against paralyzing fear. As her faith and her life's journey are lived out amidst the crushing darkness of the Nazi persecution, she becomes for us a "living image" of Christ's love. Formed and molded in her own journey of sanctity by the living images of Christ which she encountered, Stein now becomes such an image for us to follow. Arrested from her Carmelite convent on Sunday, 2 August 1942, she lives her Way of the Cross throughout the following week. She begins her final journey from Westerbork Transit Camp in the Netherlands to Auschwitz Concentration Camp on First Friday. She offers her life and passes into eternity on Sunday, 9 August 1942. In her final passion, Stein's last known words, "We are heading East," are spoken from a prison cattle car in prophetic *testimonium fidei*. Her proclamation of the ultimate victory of the Resurrection is her triumphant testament. The words of her prayer entitled "O Prince of Peace," spoken to us now from eternity, point the way:

> O my God, fill my soul with holy joy, courage, and strength to serve you. Enkindle your love in me and then walk with me along the next stretch of road before me. I do not see very far ahead, but when I have arrived where the horizon now closes down, a new prospect will open before me, and I shall meet it with peace. Amen.[117]

When we also live such a life of union with God, the perfection of the Divine Archetype pours forth through our lives to those we encounter. Our witness causes joy in beauty and transforms the souls of those God places on our path. As Pope St. John Paul II proclaims in his *Letter to Artists*:

May the beauty which you pass on to generations still to come be such that it will stir them to wonder! Faced with the sacredness of life and of the human person, and before the marvels of the universe, wonder is the only appropriate attitude.

From this wonder there can come that enthusiasm (through) which ... humanity, every time it loses its way, will be able to lift itself up and set out again on the right path. In this sense it has been said with profound insight that *"beauty will save the world."*[118]

When, as a masterpiece of the Divine Artist, our human life is an imitation of the Divine Life, an authentic manifestation of God's perfect intention for us, expressed through our union with the divine will, we too have the potential to pour out this unsurpassed splendor of divine beauty upon the world.

Notes

1. Stein, "I Am Always in Your Midst," in *The Hidden Life*, 120.
2. Edith Stein, *Finite and Eternal Being*, trans. Kurt F. Reinhardt, ed. Dr. L. Gelber and Romaeus Leuven, OCD, *The Collected Works of Edith Stein*, Vol 9 (Washington, DC: ICS Publications, 2002), 161.
3. Stein, *Finite*, 161, italics given.
4. Edith Stein, *The Science of the Cross: A Study of St. John of the Cross*, trans. Hilda Graef, ed. Dr. L. Gelber and Romaeus Leuven, OCD (London: Burns and Oates, 1960) 208, (pg. 275 in ICS Publications edition).
5. Stein, *Finite*, 165, italics given.
6. Stein, *Finite*, 160.
7. Stein, *Finite*, 160.
8. Stein, "I Am Always in Your Midst," in *The Hidden Life*, 119.
9. Stein, "Ways to Interior Silence," in *Woman*, 143.
10. Posselt, *Edith Stein*, 111.
11. Posselt, *Edith Stein*, 111–112.
12. Posselt, *Edith Stein*, 69, italics given.
13. Posselt, *Edith Stein*, 71.
14. Stein, *Woman*, 98, italics given.
15. Stein, *Finite*, 417, italics given.
16. Stein, *Finite*, 417.
17. Stein, *Woman*, 98–9.
18. Stein, *Woman*, 89.
19. Stein, *Woman*, 97, italics added.
20. Stein, *Woman*, 93–4, italics given.
21. For the complete text of the *Aufsatzthemen: Essay Themes and Exam Topics*, see Elizabeth A. Mitchell, S.C.D., *Artist and Image: Artistic Creativity and Personal Formation in the Thought of Edith Stein* (Memphis: St. Paul Institute, 2021) https://stpaulmemphis.com/product/the-artist-the-image/.
22. Stein, *Aufsatzthemen*, nos. 7–8, in Elizabeth A. Mitchell, *Artist and Image: Artistic Creativity and Personal Formation in the Thought of Edith Stein* (Memphis: St. Paul Institute, 2021) https://stpaulmemphis.com/product/the-artist-the-image/. Translation mine.
23. Stein, *Woman*, 100.
24. Stein, *Woman*, 102.

25. Stein, *Aufsatzthemen*, nos. 3–4, 5–6, 9–10, 11–12, 16, in Mitchell, *Artist and Image.* Translation mine.
26. Stein, *Woman*, 103.
27. Stein, *Woman*, 103, italics given.
28. Stein, *Woman*, 103.
29. Stein, *Woman*, 103, 107.
30. Edith Stein, *The Science of the Cross: A Study of St. John of the Cross*, trans. Josephine Koeppel, OCD, ed. Dr. L. Gelber and Romaeus Leuven, OCD, *The Collected Works of Edith Stein*, Vol. 6 (Washington, DC: ICS Publications, 2002) 11.
31. Stein, *Science*, 11.
32. Stein, *Science*, 10.
33. Stein, *Woman*, 242.
34. Stein, *Woman*, 242.
35. Stein, *Life*, 74–75.
36. Stein, *Life*, 74.
37. Stein, *Life*, 74–75.
38. Stein, *Life*, 74.
39. Stein, *Life*, 75.
40. Stein, *Life*, 75.
41. Stein, *Woman*, 231.
42. Stein, *Science*, 10.
43. Stein, *Science*, 11.
44. Stein, *Science*, 11.
45. Stein, *Science*, 10.
46. Stein, *Science*, 10.
47. Stein, *Science*, 11, italics given.
48. Stein, *Science*, 11.
49. Stein, *Science*, 13.
50. Stein, *Science*, 11.
51. Edith Stein, *Philosophy of Psychology and the Humanities*, trans. Mary Catherine Baseheart and Marianne Sawicki, ed. Marianne Sawicki, *The Collected Works of Edith Stein*, Vol. 7 (Washington DC: ICS Publications, 2000) 221.
52. Stein, *Science*, 12.
53. Stein, *Science*, 12.
54. Stein, *Science*, 38, 42.

55. Stein, *Science*, 39, italics given.
56. Stein, *Science*, 39, italics given.
57. Stein, *Science*, 40.
58. Stein, *Science*, 41.
59. Stein, *Science*, 40.
60. Stein, *Science*, 40–1.
61. Edith Stein, "Ways to Know God," *Knowledge and Faith*, trans. Walter Redmond, ed. Dr. L. Gelber and Michael Linssen, OCD, *The Collected Works of Edith Stein*, Vol. 8 (Washington, DC: ICS Publications, 2000) 124.
62. Stein, *Science*, 42.
63. Stein, "Ways to Know God," *Knowledge and Faith*, 121.
64. Stein, *Science*, 42, italics given.
65. Karol Wojtyla. *Faith According to Saint John of the Cross*. trans. Jordan Aumann, OP (San Francisco: Ignatius Press, 1981) 21.
66. Wojtyla, *Faith According to Saint John of the Cross*, 52.
67. Stein, *Science*, 238.
68. Stein, *Science*, 233.
69. Stein, *Science*, 233.
70. Stein, *Science*, 234, italics given.
71. Stein, *Science*, 42.
72. Stein, *Science*, 12, italics given.
73. Stein to Martin Farber, 4 April 1940, as noted in Edith Stein, *Knowledge and Faith*, trans. Walter Redmond, (ICS Publications: Washington, DC, 2000) xiv.
74. Stein, "Ways to Know God," *Knowledge and Faith*, 125.
75. Stein, "Ways to Know God," *Knowledge and Faith*, 124.
76. Stein, *Philosophy of Psychology*, 229.
77. Edith Stein, *On the Problem of Empathy*, trans. Waltraut Stein, Ph. D., 3rd rev. ed. The Collected Works of Edith Stein, Vol. 3, (Washington, DC: ICS Publications, 1989) 109.
78. Stein, "Ways to Know God," *Knowledge and Faith*, 100, italics given.
79. Stein, "Ways to Know God," *Knowledge and Faith*, 96, italics given.
80. Stein, "Ways to Know God," *Knowledge and Faith*, 96–7.
81. Thornton Wilder, *Our Town*, Act III, Perennial Classics edition (New York: Harper Collins, 1998), 108, italics given.
82. Stein, *Finite*, 419.
83. Stein, *Finite*, 420.

84. Stein, *Finite*, 420, italics given.
85. Stein, *Finite*, 418.
86. Edith, *Finite*, xxvii.
87. Stein, *Finite*, xxvii.
88. Stein, *Finite*, 319.
89. Stein, *Finite*, 319.
90. Stein, *Finite*, 319, note 77 (see Thomas Aquinas, *Summa Theologiae*, I/II, q. 27, a 1, ad 3, and ibid., I, q. 9 1, a 3, ad 3) italics added.
91. Stein, *Finite*, 319.
92. Stein, *Finite*, 318 (Stein's note: "Cf. Aristotle, *Metaphysics*, M 3, 1078a 30ff. In this passage Aristotle refers to 'another place' where he intends to treat more extensively of this problem. However, it is not clear what other place in his writings he may have had in mind" (*Finite*, 593, note 74).
93. Stein, *Finite*, 320.
94. Stein, *Finite*, 319, italics given.
95. Aquinas, *Summa Theologiae*, I, q. 5, a 4, ad 1, as quoted in Stein, *Finite*, 319.
96. Stein, *Finite*, 320.
97. Stein, *Finite*, 322.
98. Stein, *Finite*, 322.
99. Stein, *Finite*, 322–3 (included quote from I John 1:5).
100. Aquinas, *Summa Theologiae*, I., q. 39, a 8, *corp. art.*, as quoted in Stein, *Finite*, 322, italics given.
101. Stein, *Finite*, 322.
102. Stein, *Finite*, 323.
103. Stein, *Finite*, 323
104. Stein, *Finite*, 323 (included quote from Aquinas, *Summa Theologiae*, II/II, q. 145, a 2, *corp. art.*) italics added.
105. Stein, *Finite*, 594, note 85.
106. Stein, *Finite*, 323.
107. Stein, *Finite*, 322 (see Aquinas, *Summa Theologiae*, I, q. 39, a 8, *corp. art.*).
108. Stein, *Finite*, 322.
109. Stein, *Woman*, 200, italics added.
110. Stein, *Self-Portrait in Letters*, Letter 89 to Sr. Adelgundis Jaegerschmid, OSB.
111. Edith Stein, in *Edith Stein: Essential Writings*, John Sullivan, OCD, ed.

(Maryknoll, NY: Orbid Books, 2008) 71, italics given.
112. Stein, "Ways to Interior Silence," in *Woman*, 143.
113. Stein, "Ways to Interior Silence," in *Woman*, 143.
114. Julius Markan, in Posselt, 217.
115. Stein, *Self-Portrait in Letters*, Letter 85 to Sr. Callista Kopf, OP.
116. Stein, in Posselt, 159–160.
117. *Living with Christ*, "Prayer of St. Teresa Benedicta of the Cross (Edith Stein)," (Worchester, MA: Bayard Press, 2023) August 2023, Volume 24, No. 9.
118. John Paul II, *Letter to Artists*, n. 16, italics added. The quotation is from F. Dostoyevsky, *The Idiot*, Part III, chap. 5.

CONCLUSION

Is beauty relevant to a broken world? Can art answer the mockery of Auschwitz? Does sanctity sing against the despair of depravity? Through her vision of artistic creativity and personal formation, interwoven throughout the tapestry of her life and thought, St. Edith Stein proclaims a resounding yes. The Hand of the Divine Artist reaches the most forsaken places. His light can penetrate the interior prison of the most darkened human hearts. Our souls are made to rejoice in beauty, and we are created to radiate that beauty to the world through our lives.

Art is a lens through which St. Edith Stein sees the world and understands the human experience. She has left to us a legacy of artistic creation in her own poetic and dramatic works. Her culminating assertion that "All genuine art is revelation and all artistic creation is sacred service,"[1] proclaims her understanding of the splendor which the artwork, crafted of inanimate material or offered in living image, reveals to the world. In its congruity with the pure idea, or archetype, which the work faithfully reveals, the genuine artwork provides a glimmer of the mysterious fullness of meaning, the divine archetype which is its ultimate origin. Through such an artwork, the veil between finite and infinite is lifted, and the splendor of the eternal pours forth.

The artwork's revelation of the divine archetype, and the response which this revelation demands within our souls, lies at the heart of Stein's vision of artistic and personal formation. The beauty of the archetype radiates through created existents. The artwork which the artist creates has a formative and life-giving effect. The genuine artwork reveals the eternal and ineffable to a world too-often closed or indifferent to the beauty and splendor of divine reality.

We are not orphaned or abandoned, hopelessly lost upon the way. We can find God, Who reveals Himself through beauty, illuminating the darkness with His splendor. In his *Letter to Artists*, Pope St. John Paul II affirms this divine encounter, possible through the artwork:

> Every genuine artistic intuition goes beyond what the senses perceive and, reaching beneath reality's surface, strives to interpret its hidden mystery. The intuition itself springs from the depths of the human soul, where the desire to give meaning to one's own life is joined by the fleeting vision of beauty and of the mysterious unity of things ... Every genuine art form in its own way is a path to the inmost reality of man and of the world. It is therefore a wholly valid approach to the realm of faith, which gives human experience its ultimate meaning.[2]

Stein's vision of God and our call to sanctity culminates in the *living image*, the individual who becomes a masterpiece of the Divine Artist through grace. Through this living masterpiece, the divine archetype is communicated with a new and surpassing eloquence, and the call to the "art" of sanctity becomes a universal vocation and challenge.

Ours is a world in desperate need of beauty, a world in need of soul-awakening. We want to believe, and we hunger for hope. In living examples of heroic love, we find the strength to emulate Love itself. Stein's life witness calls us to personal holiness. From the gate of Auschwitz, from the quiet of her cloistered cell, from the academic's desk, she invites each one of us to practice the "stupendous 'art' of sanctity."[3] Her life leads us to make of our own lives a fitting response to Christ and His love. Her intercession will accompany us as we strive to transform our lives into a harmonious symphony to God's praise and glory.

In his homily at the Canonization Eucharist for Stein's elevation to sainthood in Rome, on 11 October 1998, Pope St. John Paul II fittingly declared:

Conclusion

> Throughout her life, as she grew in the knowledge of God, worshipping Him in spirit and truth, she experienced ever more clearly her specific vocation to ascend the Cross with Christ, to embrace it with serenity and trust, to love it by following in the footsteps of her beloved Spouse: St. Teresa Benedicta of the Cross is offered to us today as a model to inspire us and a protectress to call upon.
>
> We give thanks to God for this gift. May the new saint be an example to us in our commitment to serve freedom, in our search for the truth.[4]

The most profoundly moving work of art is the artwork of a human life fashioned in collaboration with the Divine Artist of creation. "Not all are called to be artists in the specific sense of the term. Yet, as Genesis has it, all men and women are entrusted with the task of crafting their own life: in a certain sense, they are to make of it a work of art, a masterpiece."[5] May our heroic love of Christ, in response to all He calls forth in us, become the "*work of art that the Spirit and our liberty create together*."[6] May each masterpiece of the Divine Artist shine forth radiantly, with St. Edith Stein, revealing that Splendor and Beauty that will transform our world.

Notes

1. Stein, *Science*, 12.
2. John Paul II, *Letter to Artists*, n. 6.
3. Pope John Paul II, "Celebrazione del Giubileo degli Artisti: Discorso," Bolletino Sala Stampa Santa Sede, 18 February 2000 (Vatican: Holy See Press Office) n. 5, translation mine.
4. Pope John Paul II, "Homily at Canonization Eucharist," in *Holiness Befits Your House: Documentation on the Canonization of Edith Stein*, ed. John Sullivan, OCD (Washington, DC: ICS Publications, 2000) n. 8.
5. John Paul II, *Letter to Artists*, n. 2, italics given.
6. Pope John Paul II, "Celebrazione del Giubileo degli Artisti: Discorso," *Bolletino Sala Stampa Santa Sede*, 18 February 2000 (Vatican: Holy See Press Office) n. 3, italics given, translation mine.

APPENDIX

MISSA IN HONOREM B.M.V. REGINAE PACIS

MASS IN HONOR OF THE BLESSED VIRGIN MARY QUEEN OF PEACE

Mass composed by St. Teresa Benedicta of the Cross at the request of her superiors, in honor of Our Lady Queen of Peace. Original text in Latin and German, with English translation provided here by the author.
Gratefully presented through the gracious permission of Sr. M. Amata Neyer, OCD, of the Edith-Stein-Archiv, Karmel Maria vom Frieden, Cologne, Germany.

Missa in honorem B. M. V. Reginae Pacis

Mass in honor of the Blessed Virgin Mary Queen of Peace

INTROITUS (GEN. 9:13)

Arcum meum ponam in nubibus, et erit signum foederis inter me et inter terram. (Ps. 28) Dominus virtutem populo suo dabit. Dominus benedicet populo suo in pace. Gloria …

Meinen Bogen will ich in die Welken setzen, und er sei zum Bundeszeichen zwischen mir und der Erde. (Ps. 28) Der Herr wird Seinem Volke Kraft verleihen, Der Herr wird Sein Volk mit Frieden segnen. Ehre …

I will place my bow in the heavens, and it will be a sign of the covenant between me and between the earth. (Ps. 28) The Lord will give strength to his people. The Lord will bless his people with peace. Glory …

+ Oratio

Deus, qui per Unigenitum tuum pacem hominibus misericorditer largiri dignatus es, concede nobis: intercedente beata Maria semper Virgine, ut tanti muneris gratia constanter perfruentes in terris, aeternae pacis gaudia consequi mereamur in caelis. Per eundem ...

O Gott, der Du in Deiner Barmherzigkeit geruhtest, durch Deinen eingeborenen Sohn den Menschen den Frieden zu schenken: gewähre uns auf die Fürbitte der seligen, allzeit jungfräulichen Maria, die Gnade, eines so großen Geschenkes auf Erden beständig zu genießen und die Freuden des ewigen Friedens im Himmel zu verdienen. Durch denselben ...

O God, who in Thy mercy deigned to give peace to men through Thine Only Begotten Son: grant to us, through the intercession of the Blessed Ever-Virgin Mary, the grace to continually enjoy such a great gift on earth and to gain the joys of eternal peace in heaven. Through the same Christ, Our Lord ...

Epistel (Gen. 9: 12–16)

Dixitque Deus: hoc signum foederis quod do inter me et vos, et ad omnem animam viventem, quae est vobiscum in generationes sempiternas: Arcum meum ponam in nubibus, et erit signum foederis inter me et inter terram. Cumque obduxo nubibus caelum, apparebit arcus meus in nubibus. Et recordabor foederis mei vobiscum, et cum omni anima vivente, quae carnem vegetat: et non erunt ultra aquae diluvii ad delendum universam carnem. Eritque arcus in nubibus, et videbo illum, et recordabor foederis sempiterni quod pactum est inter Deum et omnem animam viventem universae carnis quae est super terram.

Und Gott sprach: Dies ist das Zeichen des Bundes, den ich zwischen mir und euch errichte und für jede lebende Seele, die bei euch ist auf ewige Geschlechter: Meinen Bogen will ich in die Welken setzen, und er soll das Zeichen sein des Bundes zwischen mir und der Erde. Wenn ich den Himmel mit Wolken überziehe, wird mein Bogen in den Wolken erscheinen. Und ich werde meines Bundes mit euch gedenken und mit jeder lebenden Seele, die das Fleis belebt: und es wird fortan keine Wasserflut mehr kommen, alles Fleisch zu vertilgen. Der Bogen wird in den Wolken stehen, und ich werde ihn sehen und des ewigen Bundes gedenken, der geschlossen ward zwischen Gott und jeder lebenden Seele in allem Fleisch auf Erden.

And God said: This is the sign of the covenant which I give between me and you, and to every living soul that is with you, for perpetual generations. I will set my bow in the clouds, and it shall be the sign of a covenant between me and between the earth. And when I shall cover the sky with clouds, my bow shall appear in the clouds. And I will remember my covenant with you, and with every living soul that bears [my] flesh: and there shall be no more waters of a flood to destroy all flesh. And the bow shall be in the clouds, and I shall see it, and I shall remember the everlasting covenant that has been made between God and every living soul of all flesh that is upon the earth.

Graduale (Eccl. 43: 12–13; Apoc. 4:3)

Vide arcum, et benedic eum, qui fecit illum: valde speciosus est in splendore suo.

V. Gyravit caelum in circuitu gloriae suae, manus Excelsi aperuerunt illum.

Alleluia, alleluia.

V. Iris erat in circuitu sedis similis visionis smaragdinae. Alleluia.

Sieh den Regenbogen, und preise den, der ihn gemacht hat: gar prachtvoll ist er in seinem Glanz.

V. Er umzieht den Himmel in herrlichen Umkreis: die Hände des Allerhöchsten haben ihn ausgespannt.

Alleluja, alleluja.

V. Ein Regenbogen war ringe um den Thron, wie Smaragd anzusehen. Alleluja.

Look upon the rainbow, and bless him that made it: it is very beautiful in its brightness.

It encompasses the heaven about with the circle of its glory, the hands of the Most High have displayed it.

Alleluia, alleluia.

V. There was a rainbow round about the throne, in sight like unto an emerald.

Evangelium (Luc. 1: 26–28)

Missus est Angelus Gabriel a Deo in civitatem Galilaeae, cui nomen Nazareth, ad virginem desponsatam viro, cui nomen erat Ioseph, de domo David, et nomen virginis Maria. Et ingressus Angelus ad eam, dixit: Ave, gratia plena. Dominus tecum, benedicta tu in mulieribus.

Der Engel Gabriel ward von Gott gesandt in eine Stadt in Galilaea mit Namen Nazareth, zu einer Jungfrau die verlobt war mit einem Manne namens Joseph, aus dem Hause David, und der Name der Jungrau war Maria. Und der Engel trat zu ihe herein und sprach: Sei gegrüßt, Gnadenvelle. Der Herr ist mit dir, du bist gebenedeit unter den Frauen.

The Angel Gabriel was sent from God into a city of Galilee, called Nazareth, to a virgin espoused to a man whose name was Joseph, of the house of David; and the virgin's name was Mary. And the angel being come in, said unto her: Hail, full of grace, the Lord is with thee: blessed art thou among women.

Offertorium (Eccli. 43:12)

Vide arcum et benedic eum, qui fecit illum: valde speciosus est in splendore suo.

Siehe den Regenbogen, und preise den, der ihn gemacht hat: gar prachtvoll ist er in seinem Glanz.

Look upon the rainbow, and bless him that made it: it is very beautiful in its brightness.

Appendix

+ Secret

Hostias tibi, Domine, placationis offerimus, humiliter deprecantes, ut intercedente beata et gloriosa semper Virgine Dei Genetrice Maria, unitatis et pacis propitius dona concedes. Per Dominum nostrum …

Wir bringen Dir, o Herr, Friedopfer dar und bitten demütig: gewähre uns auf die Fürbitte der seligen und glorreichen, immer jungfräulichen Gottesgebärerin Maria gnädig die Gaben der Einigkeit und des Friedens. Durch unsern Herrn …

We offer Thee, O Lord, peace offerings, humbly beseeching Thee, that through the intercession of the blessed and glorious Mary, the Ever-Virgin Mother of God, Thou graciously bestowest the gifts of unity and peace. Through our Lord …

Communio (Gen. 9:16)

Eritque arcus in nubibus, et videbo illum, et recordabor foederis sempiterni quod pactum est inter Deum et omnem animam viventem universae carnis quae est super terram.

Der Bogen wird in den Wolken stehen, und ich werde ihn sehen und des ewigen Bundes gedenken, der geschlossen ward zwischen Gott und jeder lebenden Seele in allem Fleisch auf Erden.

And the bow shall be in the clouds, and I shall see it, and I shall remember the everlasting covenant that has been made between God and every living soul of all flesh that is upon the earth.

+ Postcommunio

Perpetuam pacem nobis, Domine, conferant sumpta mysteria, ut, intercedente beata Maria semper Virgine, liberati ab hostibus mentis et corporis in gratiarum actione iugiter maneamus. Per Dominum nostrum…

Immerwährenden Frieden mögen uns, Herr, die genossenen Geheimnisse verleihen, damit wir, auf die Fürbitte der seligen, allzeit jungfräulichen Maria von den Feinden der Seele und des

Leibes befreit, stets in Danksagung verharren. Durch unsern Herrn ...

May the mysteries we have consumed, O Lord, confer everlasting peace upon us, so that, freed from the enemies of soul and body through the intercession of the blessed ever-virgin Mary, we may constantly remain in thanksgiving. Through our Lord ...

Was mit + bezeichnet ist, haben wir aus der Messe U.Lb.Frau vom Frieden entnommen, die der Kongregation von den Heiligsten Herzen und der Ewigen Anbetung (Paris, 35, Rue de Picpus) laut Rescript vom 9. Dezember 1911 für den 9. Juli gewährt ist.

We have taken what is marked with + from the Mass of Our Lady of Peace, which was given to the Congregation of the Sacred Hearts and of Perpetual Adoration (Paris, 35, Rue de Picpus) according to the rescript of 9 December 1911, to be celebrated on July 9.

BIBLIOGRAPHY

WORKS BY STEIN

Stein, Edith. *Aufsatzthemen.* Edith-Stein-Archiv. Karmel "Maria vom Frieden." Cologne, Germany. (Published in Elizabeth A. Mitchell, *Artist and Image: Artistic Creativity and Personal Formation in the Thought of Edith Stein.* Memphis: St. Paul Institute, 2021. https://stpaulmemphis.com/product/the-artist-the-image/).

—-. *Aus dem Leben einer jüdischen Familie.* ed. Dr. L. Gelber und Romaeus Leuven, OCD. Band VII. Freiburg: Verlag Herder, 1985.

—-. *Endliches und Ewiges Sein: Versuch eines Aufstiegs zum Sinn des Seins.* ed. Dr. L. Gelber und Romaeus Leuven, OCD. Band II. Freiburg: Verlag Herder, 1986.

—-. *Erkenntnis und Glaube.* ed. Dr. L. Gelber und Romaeus Leuven, OCD. Band XV. Freiburg: Verlag Herder, 1993.

—-. *Essays on Woman.* trans. Freda Mary Oben, Ph.D. ed. Dr. L. Gelber and Romaeus Leuven, OCD. 2nd rev. ed. *The Collected Works of Edith Stein.* Vol. 2. Washington, DC: ICS Publications, 1996.

—-. *Essere Finito e Essere Eterno: Per una Elevazione al Senso dell'Essere.* trad. Luciana Vigone. ed. Dr. L. Gelber e Romaeus Leuven. Roma: Città Nuova Editrice, 1988.

—-. *Finite and Eternal Being.* trans. Kurt F. Reinhardt. ed. Dr. L. Gelber and Romaeus Leuven, OCD. *The Collected Works of Edith Stein.* Vol. 9. Washington, DC: ICS Publications, 2002.

—-. *The Hidden Life: Hagiographic Essays, Meditations, Spiritual Texts.* trans. Waltraut Stein, Ph.D. ed. Dr. L. Gelber and Romaeus Leuven, OCD. *The Collected Works of Edith Stein.* Vol. 4. Washington, DC: ICS Publications, 1992.

—-. *Knowledge and Faith.* trans. Walter Redmond. ed. Dr. L. Gelber and Michael Linssen, OCD. *The Collected Works of Edith Stein.* Vol. 8. Washington, DC: ICS Publications, 2000.

—. *Kreuzeswissenschaft: Studie über Joannes a Cruce.* ed. Dr. L. Gelber und Romaeus Leuven, OCD. Band I. Freiburg: Verlag Herder, 1983.

—. *Life in a Jewish Family.* trans. Josephine Koeppel, OCD. ed. Dr. L. Gelber and Romaeus Leuven, OCD. *The Collected Works of Edith Stein.* Vol. 1. Washington, DC: ICS Publications, 1986.

—. *Missa et Officium in Honorem B. M. V. Reginae Pacis.* Edith-Stein-Archiv. Karmel "Maria vom Frieden." Cologne, Germany. (Published in Elizabeth A. Mitchell, S.C.D. *Artist and Image: Artistic Creativity and Personal Formation in the Thought of Edith Stein.* Memphis: St. Paul Institute, 2021. https://stpaulmemphis.com/product/the-artist-the-image/).

—. *On the Problem of Empathy.* trans. Waltraut Stein, Ph.D. 3rd rev. ed. *The Collected Works of Edith Stein.* Vol. 3. Washington, DC: ICS Publications, 1989.

—. *Philosophy of Psychology and the Humanities.* trans. Mary Catherine Baseheart and Marianne Sawicki. ed. Marianne Sawicki. *The Collected Works of Edith Stein.* Vol. 7. Washington, DC: ICS Publications, 2000.

—. *The Science of the Cross.* trans. Josephine Koeppel, OCD. ed. Dr. L. Gelber and Romaeus Leuven, OCD. Washington, DC: ICS Publications, 2002.

—. *The Science of the Cross: A Study of St. John of the Cross.* trans. Hilda Graef. ed. Dr. L. Gelber and Romaeus Leuven, OCD. London: Burns and Oates, 1960.

—. *Selected Writings: With Comments and Reminiscences.* trans. and ed. Susanne Batzdorff. Springfield, Illinois: Templegate Publishers, 1990.

—. *Self-Portrait in Letters 1916–1942.* trans. Josephine Koeppel, OCD. ed. Dr. L. Gelber and Romaeus Leuven, OCD. *The Collected Works of Edith Stein.* Vol. 5. Washington, DC: ICS Publications, 1993.

—. *To Live at the Hand of the Lord: An Edith Stein Daybook.* trans. Susanne Batzdorff. ed. Sr. M. Amata Neyer, OCD. Springfield, Illinois: Templegate Publishers, 1994.

—. *Zum Problem der Einfühlung.* Inaugural-Dissertation. Universitäte zu Freiburg i. Br., 1916. Freiburg: Halle, 1917.

RELATED WORKS

Ales-Bello, Angela. "Edith Stein, a Saintly Thinker Waiting to be Discovered." *Zenit News Service*. 8 November 2002.

Aquinas, Thomas. *Introduction to St. Thomas Aquinas: The Summa Theologica, The Summa Contra Gentiles*. ed. Anton C. Pegis. Modern Library College Edition. New York: Random House, Inc., 1965.

Aristotle. *The Complete Works of Aristotle*. Revised Oxford Translation. ed. Jonathan Barnes. Vol. II. Bollingen Series LXXI. Princeton, New Jersey: Princeton University Press, 1991.

Batzdorff, Susanne M. *Aunt Edith: The Jewish Heritage of a Catholic Saint*. Springfield, Illinois: Templegate Publishers, 1998.

Butcher, S.H. *Aristotle's Theory of Poetry and Fine Art*. 4th ed. New York: Dover Publications, Inc., 1951.

Catechism of the Catholic Church. Boston: Pauline Books and Media, 1994.

Clark, Kenneth. *Civilisation*. London: Penguin Books, 1987.

Congregation for the Causes of Saints. *Positio Super Martyrio et Super Virtutibus Canonizationis Servae Dei Teresiae Benedictae a Cruce*. Roma: Tipografia Guerra, 1986.

della Croce, Giovanni, OCD. *Edith Stein: Santa Teresa Benedetta della Croce*. Milano: Mimep-Docete, 1998.

Dickens, Charles, *A Christmas Carol*. Massachusetts: Candlewick Press, 2006.

"Edith Stein." *Catholic Dossier*. Vol. 7. No. 6. Nov.-Dec. 2001. San Francisco: Ignatius Press, 2001.

Etchegaray, Cardinale Roger. "Celebrazione del Giubileo degli Artisti: Omelia." *Bollettino Sala Stampa della Santa Sede*. N. 0102. 18 February 2000. Vatican: Holy See Press Office.

de Fabrégues, Jean. *Edith Stein: Philosopher, Carmelite Nun. Holocaust Martyr*. Boston: St. Paul Books and Media, 1993.

Giron, Arthur. *Edith Stein*. New York: Samuel French, Inc., 1991.

Hardon, John, S.J. *Modern Catholic Dictionary*. Bardstown, KY: Eternal Life, 2001.

Hatem, Dr. Jad. "Il ritratto significante: la filosofia steiniana della creatività artistica." Fall Lecture Series. Rome: Pontifical University of the Holy Cross, 1999.

Herbstrith, Waltraud, OCD, ed. *Never Forget: Christian and Jewish Perspectives on Edith Stein*. trans. Susanne Batzdorff. Washington, DC: ICS Publications, 2002.

John of the Cross, St. *The Collected Works of St. John of the Cross*. trans. Kieran Kavanaugh, OCD, and Otilio Rodriguez, OCD. Washington, DC: ICS Publications, 1991.

John Paul II, Pope. "Address at Canonization Concert: Edith Stein Heard 'Melody' of God's Will." *L'Osservatore Romano*. 14 October 1998. Weekly Edition in English. No. 41.

—-. "Angelus: Edith Stein, a Beacon of Light." *L'Osservatore Romano*. 14 October 1998. Weekly Edition in English. No. 41.

—-. "Celebrazione del Giubileo degli Artisti: Discorso." *Bollettino Sala Stampa della Santa Sede*. N. 0102. 18 February 2000. Vatican: Holy See Press Office.

—-. *Ecclesia de Eucharistia*: Encyclical Letter on the Eucharist in its Relationship to the Church. Vatican City: Libreria Editrice Vaticana, 2003.

—-. "Edith Stein: Daughter of Israel, Philosopher, Carmelite, Martyr." *L'Osservatore Romano*. 14 October 1998. Weekly Edition in English. No. 41.

—-. *Letter of His Holiness Pope John Paul II to Artists*. Vatican City: Libreria Editrice Vaticana, 1999.

—-. "Master in the Faith: Apostolic Letter on the Occasion of the Fourth Centenary of the Death of St. John of the Cross." *Catholic International*. Vol. 2 No. 5. 1–14 March 1991. pp. 202–211.

—-. "Solemn Inauguration of the Special Assembly for Europe of the Synod of Bishops: Homily." 1 October 1999. Vatican. November, 2001.

Bibliography

Living with Christ, "Prayer of St. Teresa Benedicta of the Cross (Edith Stein)," (Worchester, MA: Bayard Press, 2023) August 2023, Volume 24, Number 9.

Meszaros, Marta, regia. "La Settima Stanza." Italia: Audiovisivi San Paolo, 1996.

Mitchell, Elizabeth A., S.C.D. *Artist and Image: Artistic Creativity and Personal Formation in the Thought of Edith Stein*. Rome: Edizioni Università della Santa Croce. 2004.

—-. Current print version: *Artist and Image: Artistic Creativity and Personal Formation in the Thought of Edith Stein*. Memphis: St. Paul Institute, 2021. https://stpaulmemphis.com/product/the-artist-the-image/.

—-. *Artistic Creativity and Empathic Act in the Thought of Edith Stein*. Licentiate Thesis. Pontifical University of the Holy Cross. Rome. 2000.

—-. Interview with author. February, 2002: vom Wort Gottes, Schwester Katerina (Sr. Catherine of the Word of God). Karmelitessen Klooster. Echt. Netherlands.

Neyer, Sr. Maria Amata, OCD. *Edith Stein: Her Life in Photos and Documents*. trans. Waltraut Stein, Ph.D. Washington, DC: ICS Publications, 1999.

—-. Interview with author. 8 March 2002. Karmel "Maria vom Frieden." Cologne. Germany.

Nicholls, Fr. Guy. *Unearthly Beauty: The Aesthetic of St. John Henry Newman*. Herefordshire: Gracewing, 2019.

Oben, Freda Mary, Ph.D. *The Life and Thought of St. Edith Stein*. New York: Alba House, 2001.

Payne, Steven, OCD. "Edith Stein e S. Giovanni della Croce." Fall Lecture Series. Rome: Pontifical Gregorian University, 1999.

Pieper, Josef. *Only the Lover Sings: Art and Contemplation*. trans. Lothar Krauth. San Francisco: Ignatius Press, 1990.

Posselt, Sr. Teresia Renata, OCD. *Edith Stein: The Life of a Philosopher and Carmelite*. ed. Suzanne M. Batzdorff, Josephine Koeppel, and John Sullivan. ICS Publications: Washington, DC, 2005.

Plato. *The Symposium.* trans. Christopher Gill. London: Penguin Books, 1999.

Royal, Robert. *The Catholic Martyrs of the Twentieth Century: A Comprehensive World History.* New York: The Crossroad Publishing Company, 2000.

Russell, D.A. and Michael Winterbottom. *Classical Literary Criticism.* Oxford: Oxford University Press, 1989.

Saward, John. *The Beauty of Holiness and the Holiness of Beauty: Art, Sanctity, and the Truth of Catholicism.* San Francisco: Ignatius Press, 1997.

Schüllner, Theresia. "Wortbilder: Eine Künstlerische Annäherung an Edith Stein." 26 February 2002. Ludwigshafen. Heinrich Pesch Haus.

Sullivan, John, OCD. *Holiness Befits Your House: Canonization of Edith Stein—A Documentation.* Washington, DC: ICS Publication, 2000.

Sullivan, John, OCD, ed. *Edith Stein: Essential Writings.* Maryknoll, NY: Orbid Books, 2008.

de Torre, Joseph. *Humanism and Modern Philosophy.* Philippines: The Center for Research and Communication, 1989.

Weigel, George. *Witness to Hope: The Biography of Pope John Paul II.* New York: Cliff Street Books, 1999.

Wetter, Cardinal Friedrich. "Edith Stein: Called to the Truth—Blessed by the Cross, Portrait of a Life." trans. Josephine Koeppel, OCD. Washington, DC: ICS Publications, 1998.

Wilder, Thornton. *Our Town.* Perennial Classics edition. (New York: Harper Collins, 1998).

Wojtyla, Karol. *Faith According to St. John of the Cross.* trans. Jordan Aumann, O.P. San Francisco: Ignatius Press, 1981.

Name Index

Aaron, 16
Abraham, 16–17, 20
Achilles, 105
Acutis, Blessed Carlo, 59
Agamemnon, 105
Ahasuerus, 18
Agatha, Sr. OCD, (one of Stein's convent sisters), 17
Allers, Rudolf, 117
Mother Antonia (prioress of the Echt Carmel), 18, 52
Aquinas, Saint Thomas, 8–9, 24, 112, 122, 133
Aristotle, 122, 133
Aumann, Jordan, OP, 132

Bach, Johannes Sebastian, 10–11, 79
Ballman, P., OSB, 81
Sr. Baptista, OCD, (one of Stein's convent sisters), 17
Baseheart, Mary Catherine, 131
Batzdorff, Susanne M., (niece of Edith Stein), xxi, 6, 23, 24, 51, 95
Benedict, Saint, 81
Biberstein, Doctor Erna, 6, 23
Biberstein, Ernst Ludwig, 11, 24
Biberstein, Hans, 6
Bjornssen, Bjornstjerne, 12
Böcklin, Arnold, 4, 23
Bonaparte, Napoleon, 90–91
Brüning, Mother Petra, OSU, 17, 24, 25, 95

Brutus, 105
Buonarotti, Michelangelo, xv, 67–68, 88, 93, 119

Capra, Frank, 85
Catherine of the Word of God (Katerina vom Wort Gottes), Sr., OCD, xxi, 149
Cavnar, Cynthia, xxi
Cicero, 5
Cohen, Erika, (née Tworoger, niece of Edith Stein), 6
Conrad-Martius, Hedwig, 16, 31, 34–35

David, 16, 142
de Geuser, Marie Antoinette, 16
Dickens, Charles, 70
Dionysius the Areopagite, xviii, 117
Dostoyevsky, Fyodor, 118
Dülberg, Hedwig, xxi

Eliot, T.S., 60, 92
Elijah, 16, 20
Elisha, 16
Elgar, Edward, 72
Engelmann, Mother Ambrosia Antonia, OCD, 52
Enoch, 16
Esther, Queen, 18–22, 25, 41, 112
Eszer, Fr. Ambrose, OP, 47

Fabrègues, Jean de, 2, 23
Farber, Martin, 116–117, 132
Fouqué, Valentin, 46
Francis of Assisi, 17

Gelber, Lucy, xxi, xxii, 23, 24, 51, 93, 94, 117, 130, 131, 132
Giovanni della Croce, Fr., OCD, 80, 95
Goethe, Johann Wolfgang von, 2. 66, 67, 85, 103
Graef, Hilda, 24, 51, 94, 130
Grillparzer, Franz, 3
Gretchen, (character of Goethe's Faust), 5

Haman, 18–19
Handel, George Frideric, 106
Hannibal, 84
Hardon, Fr. John, SJ, 52
Hatem, Jad, 94
Hebbel, Christian Friedrich, 3
Homer, 68, 80, 98–99, 105
Horace, 5
Husserl, Edmund, xvii, 8–10. 24, 31, 56, 80, 112

Ibsen, Heinrich, 3, 66–67, 103
Iphigenie, 105
Isaac, 16

Jacob, 16
Jaegerschmid, Sr. Adelgundis, OSB, 52, 133
Jans, Anton, 24
Joan of Arc, Saint, 16

John of the Cross, Saint, xvi, xxi, 16, 24, 51, 75–76, 94, 96, 98, 111, 115, 130, 131, 132, 136
John Paul II, Saint, xvi, xix, xxi, xxii, 52, 77, 81, 94, 115, 128, 134, 136, 138 (see also Wojtyła, Karol)
John the Baptizer, 17
John the Evangelist, 13

Kardaras, Nicholas, 93
Kaufmann, Fritz, 93, 117
Koeppel, Josephine, OCD, xxii, 23, 24, 51, 93, 94, 131
Kolbe, Maximilian, Saint, 110
Kopf, Sr. Callista, OP, 134
Klärchen, (character of Goethe's Egmont), 5

Laubhardt, Sr. Placida, OSB, 46
Leuven, Romaeus, OCD, xxi, 23, 24, 51, 93, 94, 130, 131
Linssen, Michael, OCD, xxii, 23, 132,
Livy, 8, 84
Luther, Martin, 79

Mary (the Blessed Mother), xii, xviii, 21, 29, 43, 47, 67, 126, 139–144
Mary Magdalene, 13
Markan, Julius, 126
Marley, Jacob, 70
Martin of Tours, Saint, 34–35
Marx, Olga, 15
Mascagni, Pietro, 72
Merici, Saint Angela, 27

Name Index

Mitchell, Elizabeth A., xi, xiii, xxii, 25, 95, 130, 131
Moses, 16–17
Mozart, Wolfgang Amadeus, 106
Myron, 24

Napoleon, 90–91
Newman, Saint John Henry, 30–51, 98
Neyer, Sr. M. Amata, OCD, xviii, 13, 24, 25, 45, 46, 52, 53, 104, 139
Nicholls, Fr. Guy, 30–31, 51
Nicodemus, 13
Noah, 16

Oben, Freda Mary, 17, 25, 47, 51, 52, 53, 93

Paul, Saint, xi, xix, 98, 100
Payne, Steven, OCD, 23, 52
Petrus, Pater, 16
Pieper, Josef, 63, 93
Pius XI, Pope, 41
Posselt, Sr. Teresia Renata, OCD, xvii, xxi, 24, 34, 43, 51, 52, 53, 92, 130, 134
Puccini, Giacomo, 106

Redmond, Walter, 23, 132
Reinach, Adolf, 12, 31, 33, 62
Reinach, Anna, 32, 33–34, 62
Reinach, Pauline, 12
Reinhardt, Kurt F., 51, 130
Richter, Ludwig, 4, 23
Rousseau, Jean Jacques, 85
Royal, Robert, 49, 53
Rubens, Peter Paul, 106

Sachs, Lotte, 11, 24
Saward, John, xviii, xxii
Sawicki, Marianne, 131
Scheler, Max, 31
Schiller, Friedrich, 2, 3, 108
Schwind, Canon Josef, 35, 36, 46
Scrooge, Ebenezer, 70
Shakespeare, William, 3, 69, 78, 105
Stein, Elfriede, 42 (see also Frieda Stein)
Stein, Else, 3, 39
Stein, Erna, 2, 6, 23, 38, 39 (see also Biberstein, Doctor Erna)
Stein, Frau 5, 7, 14, 15
Stein, Frieda, 9
Stein, Gerhard, 13
Stein, Paul, 9, 42
Stein, Rosa, 39, 42, 43, 47–49
Stein, Waltraut, 7, 66, 110
Stein, Wolf, 13
Sullivan, John, 5, 38, 125
Svensson, Jan

Teresa de Spiritu Sancto, 2 (see also Posselt, Sr. Teresia Renata, OCD)
Teresa of Avila, Saint, 36, 38, 44, 54
Teresa of Calcutta, Saint, 108
Thannisch, Mother Ottilia, OCD, 45
Thérèse of Lisieux, Saint, 24, 65

Undset, Sigrid, 68, 100

van Breda, Fr. Hermann, OFM, 4

van Weersth, Mother Johanna, OCD, 76
Veronica, (character of Gertrud von le Fort's Veronica's Veil), 22
von Goethe, Johann Wolfgang, 68, 86, 100
von Haller, Albrecht, 86

von le Fort, Gertrud, 21–23

Walzer, Abbot Raphael, OSB
Wilder, Thornton, 118–19
Wojtyła, Karol, 117 (see also John Paul II, Saint)
Wren, Sir Christopher, 87

Place Index

Auschwitz, xi, xv–xvi, 1, 45–47, 50, 62, 101, 110, 128, 135, 136

Bad Bergzabern, 34–35
Beuron, 80
Breslau, 4, 7, 11, 15, 79

Cologne (Köln), xii, xvi–xviii, 12, 13, 15–17, 21, 34, 39, 42–43, 47, 66, 80, 104

Echt, xii, xiii, 17–18, 27, 40–45, 116

Frankfurt, 12, 32
Freiburg, 7, 80

Göttingen, 7, 12, 31

Hamburg, 3
Hooghalen, 47

Münster, 101

Schifferstadt, 46
Speyer, 106

Westerbork, 45, 47, 126, 128

Theme Index

Aesthetics, xi, xii, xviii, 4, 30, 56, 75, 76, 80–81, 84–85, 89, 105, 106, 117, 123, and passim

Archetype, 73–74, 77, 87–90, 119, 120–121, 124–125, 128, 135–136

Architecture, 85,

Art, the artist, xi-xii, 3–6, 8, 12–13, 14, 16–18, 27–29, 66–68, 71–78, 82–83, 85–91, 97, 100, 102, 107, 109, 111–116, 119–120, 124–125, 128–129, 135–137

Artwork, xi, xiv-xv, 27–30, 55, 66–67, 71–78, 82–83, 86–91, 97, 100, 102, 111, 114, 116–119, 135–137

Beauty, xi-xiii, xvi-xviii, 1, 4, 28–31, 55–58, 71–74, 76–78, 80–82, 84, 89, 97, 102, 104–106, 113, 115, 116, 121–126, 128–129, 135–137

Blessed Mother, (see also Our Lady, Mary, Blessed Virgin)

Blessed Virgin, (see also Our Lady, Mary, Blessed Mother)

Cathedral, 28–29, 32, 76–77, 82–83, 85

Canonization, xvi, xix, xxi, xxii, 37, 40, 47, 49, 80,

Civilization, 82–86, 106

Child[ren], formation and care of, xv, 1, 2, 6, 11, 47, 49, 104–110, 111, 126–127

Clarity, as a characteristic of beauty, 87, 124–125

Community, 70, 81, 82–86

Convert, conversion xvi, 1, 6, 13–14, 31, 35, 38, 40, 43, 44, 48, 56, 80, 110

Creativity, xi, xvii-xviii, 9, 28, 56, 67–68, 86, 112–113, 119–121, 135

Cross, xi, xv-xvi, xix-xx, 1, 15, 19–21, 30, 32–34, 37, 41–42, 45, 47, 50, 56, 62, 67, 71, 74–76, 98, 106, 110–113, 128, 137

Despair, depression, 60–62, 72, 79, 127–128. 135

Dialogue, 8–9, 18, 27, 109, 112

Divine Artist, xi, xv, xix-xx, 27–29, 91, 100, 119–120, 125, 129, 135–137

Divine Will, 36, 39, 64, 100, 125–126, 129

Drama, xvi, 3, 5, 7, 8, 9–10, 16–17, 18–21, 27, 68, 69, 87, 106, 108–109, 112, 135

Education, 36, 102–106

Empathy, xi, xviii, 60, 65–68, 70

Essence, essential truth, xix, 68, 90–91, 97–99, 110, 121

Genuine Art, (see also Art, Artwork), xii, xv, xviii, 71, 74, 87, 91, 111, 116, 135–136
Grace, xix, 20, 27, 30–31, 36–37, 63–64, 100, 103, 120, 124–126, 136
Gregorian chant, 10, 80
God, as Divine Artist, xi, xv, xix-xx, 27–29, 91, 100, 119–120, 125, 129, 135–137
Goodness, xv, 97, 105, 123–125

Harmony, 29, 30, 122, 124–125
History, 6, 8, 77, 105, 110, 112–113
Holiness, 28, 30–31, 36, 37, 46, 75,-76, 98, 99, 107, 136
Holocaust, as vocation, 38, 40, 46
Holocaustum, (see also Self-offering), 40, 46

Intercession, 19, 136,
Image, (see Living Image)
Isolation, 83–84

Joy, 2, 28, 55, 56, 58, 86, 106, 110, 121–123, 128, 140

Living image, xv, xz, 13, 14, 27–28, 30–34, 37, 41, 73–77, 111–116, 118–121, 125, 135–136
Literature, 1–3, 6–8, 12, 14, 17, 33, 66–72, 78–79, 87–91, 103–105, 109, 115,
Liturgy, xviii, 21–22, 80–81

Martyr/Martyrdom, xi-xiii, xvi, 2, 37, 40–41, 47–50, 109–110, 128
Masterpiece, xi, xii, xv, xix, 27, 88–89, 9, 97, 119, 125–129, 136–137
Mary, the Blessed Virgin, xiv, 21, 29, 43, 67, 126, 139–144
Museum, 4, 12, 32
Music, xviii, 10, 16, 17, 69, 71–73, 76, 78–80, 82, 105, 112, 114, 116–117

Nature, natural world, 4, 70, 86
National Socialism/Nazis, xi, xvi, xvii, 12, 18, 38, 40–44, 48–49, 85–86, 117, 128
Night (as spiritual image for John of the Cross and Stein), 18–21, 36–37, 101, 112–115

Order/proportion as a quality of beauty, 122–123

Painting, 4, 16, 17, 75–76, 90–91, 105–106, 111, 118–120
Phenomenology, 8–9, 31–32, 56, 116–117, 121–122
Philosophy, xiii, xvi, xviii, 3, 6–9, 16, 30–31, 38, 55–56, 86, 112, 121–122
Pietà, xv, 67, 119
Poetry, xi, 2, 3, 6, 17, 28, 31, 60, 71–72, 77,84, 88–89, 103, 109, 111–113, 116, 117
Portraiture, (see Painting)
Providence, 35, 126

Theme Index

Pure idea, (see also Archetype), 72–74, 86–92, 135

Radiance, 30, 121, 124–125
Reading, 2–3, 10, 22, 44, 69, 79, 108
Receptivity, 57, 64–65, 77, 86, 107, 110, 113
Realism, 107, 109–113, 116
Resting in God, 64–65
Revelation, xii, xv, xviii, 18, 28, 73–74, 77, 86–88, 90, 116, 124–125, 135
Rhapsodic Theater, xvi

Sacrifice, xi, xii, xx, 20–21, 40–41, 46–48, 62, 72, 101, 110, 128
Sanctity, xi, xii, xvi, xix, 30, 40, 47–48, 74, 101, 124–125, 128, 135–136
Science (of the Cross), xii, xv-xvi, xviii, xxi, xxii, 30, 56, 62, 71, 74, 76, 98, 110–111
Sculpture, 12–13, 17, 32, 119
Self-Offering, (see also Holocaustum), xv, 1, 41, 110, 112
Sign, 30, 31, 42, 112, 139, 141

Soul, as channel of God's splendor, 29–30, 31, 55–64, 71–73, 76–77, 102–104, 106–107, 110, 113, 124–125, 127–128
Splendor, xii, xv, 30, 55–56, 77, 124–125, 128–129, 135–137
Storytelling, 11
Surrender, xi, xx, 22, 36, 38, 64, 76, 97, 100, 126–127
Symbol, symbolism, xi, xvi, xviii, 73, 112–118
Symphony, xix-xx, 127, 136

Teacher (Stein as teacher), 35, 101, 104–106, 109
Theater, xvi, 7, 10, 104, 108
Truth, xi-xii, xv-xvi, 28, 34, 37–38, 40, 50, 62, 73, 79, 90–91, 105, 114, 123–124

Vocation, 7, 18, 31–33, 36, 127, 136–137

Witness, of faith,, xi, xii, xvi, xx, 13, 31, 34, 38–40, 43, 47, 49–50, 102, 115, 128, 136
Woman, vocation of, 36, 66–67, 103, 107, 126

www.ingramcontent.com/pod-product-compliance
Lightning Source LLC
Chambersburg PA
CBHW022103160426
43198CB00008B/334